Understanding Race, Class, Gender, and Sexuality: Case Studies

Understanding Race, Class, Gender, and Sexuality:

CASE STUDIES

Lynn Weber

Heather Dillaway

Boston   Burr Ridge, IL   Dubuque, IA   Madison, WI   New York
San Francisco   St. Louis   Bangkok   Bogotá   Caracas   Kuala Lumpur
Lisbon   London   Madrid   Mexico City   Milan   Montreal   New Delhi
Santiago   Seoul   Singapore   Sydney   Taipei   Toronto

McGraw-Hill Higher Education ✖

*A Division of The **McGraw-Hill** Companies*

This book is printed on acid-free paper.

1 2 3 4 5 6 7 8 9 0 FGR/FGR 0 9 8 7 6 5 4 3 2 1

ISBN 0-07-243463-5

Editorial director: *Phillip A. Butcher*
Sponsoring editor: *Sally Constable*
Developmental editor: *Katherine Blake*
Project manager: *Laura Griffin*
Manager, new book production: *Melonie Salvati*
Designer: *Matthew Baldwin*
Cover designer: *Adam Rooke*
Cover image: *Diana Ong/SuperStock*
Compositor: *Shepherd Incorporated*
Typeface: *10/12 Palatino*
Printer: *Quebecor World Fairfield Inc.*

Library of Congress Card Number: 2001086068

www.mhhe.com

CONTENTS

ABOUT THE AUTHORS

LYNN WEBER has been the Director of Women's Studies and a Professor of Sociology at the University of South Carolina since 1996. She arrived at South Carolina after serving two years as Distinguished Professor in Race, Class, and Gender at the University of Delaware and having spent the previous 13 years co-founding and later directing the Center for Research on Women at the University of Memphis.

Founded in 1982 by Weber, Bonnie Thornton Dill, and Elizabeth Higginbotham, the Center for Research on Women was the first in the nation to focus on women of color and on the intersections of race, class, and gender. Over the years, Weber—in conjunction with many scholars associated with the Center—provided pioneering scholarship on race, class, and gender and served as a leader in innovative teaching and curriculum change focused on race, class, and gender. Many of today's leading race, class, and gender scholars have been deeply involved with the work of the Center, serving on the faculty, on the advisory board, as visiting scholars, and as curriculum workshop leaders and participants. These scholars include Patricia Hill Collins, Maxine Baca Zinn, Evelyn Nakano Glenn, Judith Rollins, Esther Chow, Elaine Bell Kaplan, Cheryl Gilkes, Kenneth Goings, Sharon Harley, Leith Mullings, Sandra Morgen, Kathy Ward, Denise Segura, Ruth Zambrana, Mary Romero, Bernice Barnett, Sheryl Ruzek, and many others. For the pioneering research of the Center, Weber, Dill, and Higginbotham received the Jessie Bernard Award of the American Sociological Association in 1993, and for innovative pedagogical work, they received the ASA's Distinguished Contributions to Teaching Award in the same year—a dual honor never bestowed before or since.

Co-author of *The American Perception of Class*, Weber has published on the intersections of race, class, and gender—especially in the process of upward social mobility, in mental health, and in the lives of professional-managerial women. In addition, she has published articles on teaching race, class, and gender, including the lead article, "A Conceptual Framework for Understanding Race, Class, Gender, and Sexuality," in a recent special issue of *Psychology of Women Quarterly* devoted to teaching about gender and ethnicity. Weber is the author of the new groundbreaking text *Understanding Race, Class, Gender, and Sexuality: A Conceptual Framework* (McGraw-Hill, 2001).

Weber has consulted with many higher education institutions of all types on ways to integrate race, class, and gender into the curriculum. Her special focus has been on classroom dynamics and ways to convey difficult and potentially volatile material so that learning is enhanced.

HEATHER DILLAWAY received her master's degree in sociology from the University of Delaware in 1997. She is currently a PhD candidate at Michigan State University. Most of her written work, presentations, and publications have dealt with the connections between reproductive experiences and inequality. She is currently working on a dissertation covering women's experiences with menopause and how this reproductive experience is affected by women's social locations (race, class, gender, sexuality, family situation, etc.). Her major areas of interest include race, class, gender, and sexuality studies, sociology of the family (in particular, the sociology of motherhood/fatherhood), sociology of reproduction, and women's health. Dillaway has taught many sociology courses in the past five years, including sociology of sex and gender, introduction to women's studies, sociology of the family, and social stratification. In her teaching, Dillaway, like Weber, integrates a race, class, gender, and sexuality lens into the college curriculum.

PREFACE

The eight case studies presented in this book are to be used to analyze race, class, gender, and sexuality dynamics in the United States today. To facilitate analysis, each case is accompanied by a set of questions addressing the five themes in the conceptual framework presented in Lynn Weber's text *Understanding Race, Class, Gender, and Sexuality: A Conceptual Framework*, which is also published by McGraw-Hill. The Introduction to these cases provides a summary of Weber's conceptual framework.

These cases have been carefully selected to represent a wide range of group experiences cross-cutting

— race, class, gender, and sexuality
— institutional arenas
— regional locations
— thematic foci.

In each case, the reader is asked to analyze both the foregrounded and the less apparent dimensions of oppression and privilege. Questions help to guide interrogations within the five themes of the framework. Questions also ask students to consider the implications for social action and social justice embedded in the stories and their analyses.

DISTINGUISHING FEATURES

- The cases are primary, unanalyzed narratives and first-person accounts—not mere secondary analyses about oppression.
- The limited number of cases presented allows for greater depth of analysis than is typically possible using a longer anthology.
- The cases highlight the complexities and interrelations of the dimensions of oppression and privilege.
- Questions *guide* the reader toward complex and critical analysis; they do not prescribe it for the reader.

- The stories presented involve a diverse group of people across race, class, gender, sexuality, age, disability, region, and timeframe, as well as diverse themes in criminal justice, education, family, work and economy, masculinity and femininity, identity, the American Dream, collective action, and the state.
- Each story addresses multiple intersections of inequalities and yet, taken together, the stories weave a web that even more powerfully illustrates complex interactions of race, class, gender, and sexuality.

ACKNOWLEDGMENTS

Since this book of case studies was developed in conjunction with *Understanding Race, Class, Gender, and Sexuality: A Conceptual Framework,* all of the people who contributed in multiple ways to the development of the text also contributed to the development of this book of case studies.

Elizabeth Higginbotham and Tina Hancock participated in initial brainstorming sessions for framing the text and for incorporating case studies as a way to best advance analyses of the intersections of race, class, gender, and sexuality. Lynn Weber's graduate research assistants at the University of South Carolina—Shannon Hunnicutt, Rebecca Shrum, and Kerry McLoughlin—made significant contributions to the text in numerous ways. Shannon, Rebecca, and Kerry have meticulously researched almost every topic in the books, have given valuable critiques, and have done the serious work of checking every reference, every detail. These books have been greatly improved by their involvement.

Over the last six years, students in Lynn Weber's seminars on race, class, gender, and sexuality and her seminars in women's studies at the University of Delaware and the University of South Carolina, and students in Heather Dillaway's gender, family, and social stratification courses at Michigan State University have read and given invaluable feedback on the latest iterations of the text and case studies. We thank them for seriously engaging in these projects and for the many good suggestions they made.

Several colleagues read the manuscript and gave detailed and enormously helpful critiques—Judith Barker, Kathleen Blee, Craig Kridel, Mary Margaret Fonow, Joan Spade, Susan Spivey, Kathy Ward, and Bruce Williams. Bonnie Thornton Dill not only read the manuscript but also used a draft in her women's studies seminar on power and conflict at the University of Maryland. Maxine Baca Zinn has generously provided critical feedback and assistance in many ways—from recommending readings to theoretical critique to providing insights on the publication process. We are grateful to Maxine and to Bonnie and her students for their critical vision and many good suggestions. We are also indebted to the staff at the University of South Carolina Women's Studies program, Rosa Thorn and Jackie McClary, for the many ways in which they facilitated the project.

Finally, our families and friends have supported us in more ways than we can name. Chris, Russ, Annie, and Kate Bohner have engaged in numerous discussions of the issues and themes contained in these books and have always given thoughtful and honest feedback. Jean Bohner provided not only encouragement but also critical feedback and edited every line of both books. Jason Brater contributed unending support and assurance for Heather Dillaway and acted as a valuable sounding board at critical junctures during the creation of this case study book. We are deeply grateful to each of them.

Lynn Weber
University of South Carolina
Heather Dillaway
Michigan State University

INTRODUCTION

From the time that Lynn Weber began to work on *Understanding Race, Class, Gender, and Sexuality: A Conceptual Framework*, she knew that she wanted to use real life vignettes—case studies—to convey the framework. Conducting research and teaching about race, class, gender, and sexuality for many years had taught her that analyses must be grounded in real life experience to reveal the intersecting dynamic relationships of these hierarchies of inequality. Further, as most of the anthologies on the topic demonstrate, beginning with personal experience is perhaps the best way to engage the reader in analyses of these complex intersections. So throughout that text, extensive examples and case studies are used to illustrate the themes of the conceptual framework for analyzing the intersections of race, class, gender, and sexuality.

THE CONCEPTUAL FRAMEWORK

In this book of case studies, Heather Dillaway and Lynn Weber provide you with an opportunity to conduct your own analyses of race, class, gender, and sexuality systems—to think critically about the ways that these multiple systems simultaneously operate in every social relationship, in every social institution from the economy to the family, and in every person's sense of who he or she is. To help guide your analysis, we provide questions that are organized by the themes in the conceptual framework. These themes were culled from many works published in the last 20 years that sought to analyze intersecting race, class, gender, and sexuality systems in ways that

- are complex—not superficial and simplistic—and incorporate multiple dimensions of inequality in the same analysis

1

- do not seek to rank the dimensions of inequality according to which one represents the greatest oppression, which group has suffered the most
- empower—further the cause of social and economic justice by providing understanding and insights that lead to challenging injustice effectively.

The five themes are described in detail in *Understanding Race, Class, Gender, and Sexuality: A Conceptual Framework* but are briefly summarized here. Some general questions are also provided to serve as guides or starting places for exploring how each theme identifies a critical dimension of race, class, gender, and sexuality systems of inequality and therefore of any analysis of them.

Theme 1: Historically and Geographically/ Globally Contextual

Race, class, gender, and sexuality can be understood only in their *historical and geographic/global contexts*. So analyses focus on specific times and places and avoid the search for common meanings of race, class, gender, and sexuality that would apply in all times and places. When we examine situations, it is important to know the histories and global contexts of particular groups so that we can come to understand their current situations and their interpretations of events. Taking a broad historical and global view also enables us to see the tremendous changes that have taken place in each of these systems over time and the diversity across social geography and to recognize the potential for change in situations we face every day. When analyzing the case studies and events in your own life, ask:

- How have the relevant ideologies, the controlling images, developed over time? In this location? In other locations?
- What political processes have shaped this situation over time? In this location? In other locations?
- What historical economic conditions have affected the situation? What regional economic conditions? What global economic conditions?
- How would this situation be understood at a different historical time? In different regional and geographic locations?

Theme 2: Socially Constructed

Race, class, gender, and sexuality are *social constructs* whose meanings develop out of group struggles over socially valued resources. While they may have biological or material referents, race, class, gender, and sexuality are not fixed properties of individuals nor of materially defined groups. Their meaning can and does change over time and in different social contexts. Ask:

- Are race, class, gender, and sexuality taken to determine how people should be—out of some notion of biological imperative or of inherent inferiority?
- Are race, class, gender, and sexuality seen as immutable "facts" of people's lives or of social situations?

- Are people's economic resources, power, prestige, education, health—their total status—seen as something they earned through individual effort?
- How might the situation be viewed differently by people in different race, class, gender, and sexuality social locations?

Theme 3: Power Relationships

Race, class, gender, and sexuality are *power relationships of dominance and subordination,* not merely gradations along a scale of resources—who has more than whom—or differences in cultural preferences or gender roles. They are based in relationships of exploitation of subordinate groups by dominant groups for a greater share of society's valued resources. These relationships change because oppressed groups struggle to gain rights, opportunities, and resources and to gain greater control over their lives from dominant groups that seek to maintain their position of control over the political, ideological, and economic social domains—over their own lives as well as over others' lives.

Try not to confuse personal power with social power. Individuals can be powerful by virtue of their insight, knowledge, personalities, and other traits. They can persuade others to act in ways they want. And this personal power can be achieved in spite of a lack of socially institutionalized power. It is the social power that accrues from occupying a position of dominance in the race, class, gender, and sexuality systems that we seek to understand here. Ask:

- What are the institutional arrangements that benefit the powerful and cost others in this situation?
- Which group(s) gain and which group(s) lose in the institutional arrangements we observe?
- Have the participants come to believe (internalized) that they lack power or have power in the situation? How have their beliefs affected their actions?

Theme 4: Macro/Social Structural and Micro/Social Psychological Levels

These power relationships between dominant and subordinate groups are embedded in society's *macro* social institutions and in the *micro* face-to-face interactions that constitute the everyday lives of individuals. Specifying the linkages between these two levels is a key component of a race, class, gender, and sexuality analysis. When you analyze a particular social event, seeing the interpersonal and psychological manifestations of oppression is often easy. But because the broad macro-level forces that shape events are more remote and abstract, they are more difficult to see. Ask:

- Which group(s) are empowered and which group(s) are disempowered in the macro institutional arrangements we observe?
- What are the ideological, political, and economic institutional arrangements and practices that are shaping each actor's actions and views in the situation?

- Imagine changes in key macro institutional conditions, such as the onset of an economic recession or a change in laws. How would these changes alter the situation?
- How does each of the actors view the situation? Is that view different for people in different race, class, gender, and sexuality locations?
- Are oppressed group members aware of the race, class, gender, and sexuality power structures in the situation? Is there evidence that they resist controlling images in their views and their actions? Is there evidence that they have accepted the controlling images, the limits on their lives? Why?
- Are dominant group members aware of their privilege in the situation? What does it mean to them? What views do they hold of oppressed groups? If they do not take oppressed groups into account, why not?

Theme 5: Simultaneously Expressed

Race, class, gender, and sexuality *simultaneously operate* in every social situation. At the societal level, these systems of social hierarchies are connected to each other and are embedded in all social institutions. At the individual level, we each experience our lives based on our location along *all* dimensions, so we may occupy positions of dominance and subordination at the same time. Ask yourself about all of the systems operating in every situation you examine. Although one may appear to be in the foreground, go behind the obvious and ask about the less visible dimensions:

- If we take account of only a single dimension of oppression (e.g., gender) and ignore the others, how might we interpret the situation differently?
- What are the dimensions that are foregrounded, that are fairly obvious, in this situation?
- What are the dimensions that are not as apparent? Why?
- How does the power of the individuals involved shape our perspective on what dimensions are important?

Implications for Social Action and Social Justice

Finally, when conducting race, class, gender, and sexuality analyses, it is important to be explicit about what you hope to gain through such analyses. Ask yourself about the implications for social justice of the perspective you have, the questions you ask, and the answers you obtain:

- Do your analyses provide insights that in a political context would likely serve to reinforce existing power relations?
- Do your analyses illuminate processes of resistance or avenues for self-definition or self-valuation that could transform the race, class, gender, and sexuality hierarchies?
- How might people in different social locations react to and employ your analyses? To what ends?

QUESTIONS FOR ANALYSIS

Accompanying each of the eight case studies presented here is a set of specific questions associated with each of the five themes in the framework as well as questions about the implications of the case for social action and social justice. These questions are not intended to be comprehensive and to touch on every possible avenue one could pursue in attempting to understand each thematic aspect of race, class, gender, and sexuality systems. Furthermore, they are not organized in a linear progression. Instead, they are intended as questions to spur critical thought about the multiple dimensions of each of these systems as well as of their intersecting dynamics. Because each of us brings to an analysis the knowledge and perspectives that have been shaped by our own social location in race, class, gender, and sexuality hierarchies, our analyses will likely take many directions as different people are better situated to see the dynamics of inequality in different aspects of stories or situations. Thus, bringing multiple angles of vision to bear on any case will certainly enrich and likely change any analysis.

Although the questions are organized by conceptual theme, you will also find that there is considerable overlap in the themes that need to be addressed to answer any specific question and that some of the questions might thus fit into several of the themes. Just as race, class, gender, and sexuality as systems intersect, so do the conceptual themes that undergird these systems connect and overlap. For example, the fact that the meanings of race, class, gender, and sexuality are historically, geographically, and globally contextual in many ways implies that they are socially constructed and thus can and do change over time and place. Likewise, that they are power relationships merely specifies that the relationships are of dominance and subordination, yet these relationships take place at both the macro/social structural and micro/social psychological levels. And the simultaneous expression of race, class, gender, and sexuality inequalities is manifest as we explore all of the other themes. So use the questions to spur your thinking to generate complex, dynamic, and useful analyses of the intersections of race, class, gender, and sexuality in specific social situations and in specific lives.

ABOUT THE CASES

The eight case studies presented here were selected for several reasons. First, we wanted to present a range of different experiences across multiple social locations and yet to do so in only a few cases. Consequently, considerable race, class, gender, and sexuality diversity is represented in these cases. But they are by no means comprehensive or exhaustive. The stories involve

- native born and immigrant populations
- multiple racial groups including people of African, Asian, European, Mexican, and Native descent

- poor, working-class, and middle-class people
- gays, lesbians, bisexuals, and heterosexuals
- men and women.

They also include

- rural, suburban, and urban dwellers
- a wide age range
- regional variation (Northeast, South, Southwest, and Midwest)
- international variation.

Major political, economic, and ideological institutions are highlighted across the eight studies

- federal and state government agencies and organizations
- the economy and workforce
- marriage and the family
- education
- law and criminal justice.

Likewise, the studies problematize dominant ideologies such as the American Dream, heterosexuality, masculinity and femininity, and Whiteness.

RESOURCES

To facilitate your analyses of race, class, gender, and sexuality systems, we provide a few references at the end of each case. And this introduction is followed by a set of general references that might be useful in each of the cases. You may also wish to refer to Lynn Weber's (2001) *Understanding Race, Class, Gender, and Sexuality: A Conceptual Framework*, New York: McGraw-Hill, which provides not only a fuller discussion of the framework but also a detailed time line of indicators of oppression and resistance in modern U.S. history. Finally, this introduction is also followed by a list of current anthologies on race, class, gender, and sexuality that can be resources as well as opportunities for conducting further analyses.

GENERAL REFERENCES

Abramovitz, Mimi. 1996. *Regulating the Lives of Women: Social Welfare Policy from Colonial Times to the Present*. Boston, MA: South End Press.

Baca Zinn, Maxine. 1998. *Diversity in Families*. New York: Longman.

——— 2000. Michael A. Messner and Pierrette Hondagneu-Sotelo (Eds.). *Gender through the Prism of Difference*, Second Edition. Boston, MA: Allyn & Bacon.

Bondi, Victor (Ed.). 1994. *American Decades*. Volumes 1–9. Detroit, MI: Gale Research, Inc.

Bradley, David and Shelley Fisher Fishkin. 1998. *The Encyclopedia of Civil Rights in America*. Volumes 1–3. New York: Sharpe Reference.

Ferguson, Susan J. 1997. *Shifting the Center: Understanding Contemporary Families*. Mountain View, CA: Mayfield.

Gall, Susan and Irene Natividad (Eds.). 1993. *The Asian American Almanac: A Reference Work on Asians in the United States*. Detroit, MI: Gale Research, Inc.

Hine, Darlene Clark (Ed.). 1993. *Black Women in America: An Historical Encyclopedia*. Brooklyn, NY: Carlson.

Kanellos, Nicolas (Ed.). 1993. *The Hispanic American Almanac: A Reference Work on Hispanics in the United States*. Detroit, MI: Gale Research, Inc.

——— 1997. *Hispanic Firsts: 500 Years of Extraordinary Achievement*. Detroit, MI: Gale Research, Inc.

Salzman, Jack, David Lionel Smith, and David West (Eds.). 1996. *Encyclopedia of African American Culture and History*. Volumes 1–5. New York: Simon and Schuster.

Shinagawa, Larry Hajime and Michael Jang. 1998. *Atlas of American Diversity*. Walnut Creek, CA: AltaMira Press.

Skolnick, Arlene S. and Jerome H. Skolnick. 1999. *Family in Transition*. New York: Longman.

Takaki, Ronald (Ed.). 1994. *From Different Shores: Perspectives on Race and Ethnicity in America*. New York: Oxford University Press.

Vecoli, Rudolph J. (Ed.). 1995. *Gale Encyclopedia of Multicultural America*. Volumes 1–2. Detroit, MI: Gale Research, Inc.

ANTHOLOGIES

Andersen, Margaret L. and Patricia Hill Collins (Eds.). 2001. *Race, Class, and Gender: An Anthology*. Belmont, CA: Wadsworth.

Anzaldúa, Gloria (Ed.). 1990. *Making Face, Making Soul, Haciendo Caras: Creative and Critical Perspectives by Feminists of Color*. San Francisco, CA: Aunt Lute Foundation Books.

Beemyn, Brett (Ed.). 1997. *Creating a Place for Ourselves: Lesbian, Gay and Bisexual Community Histories*. New York: Routledge.

Booth, Alan, Ann C. Crouter, and Nancy Landale (Eds.). 1997. *Immigration and the Family: Research and Policy on U.S. Immigrants*. Mahwah, NJ: Lawrence Erlbaum Associates.

Brandt, Eric (Ed.). 1999. *Dangerous Liaisons: Blacks, Gays, and the Struggle for Equality*. New York: New Press.

Cyrus, Virginia (Ed.). 2000. *Experiencing Race, Class, and Gender in the United States*. 3rd Edition. Mountain View, CA: Mayfield.

Delgado, Richard and Jean Stefancic (Eds.). 1997. *Critical White Studies: Looking Behind the Mirror*. Philadelphia: Temple Press.

Disch, Estelle (Ed.). 1997. *Reconstructing Gender: A Multicultural Anthology*. Mountain View, CA: Mayfield.

Ferguson, Susan. 1999. *Mapping the Social Landscape: Readings in Sociology.*
    Mountainview, CA: Mayfield.
Higginbotham, Elizabeth and Mary Romero (Eds.). 1997. *Women and Work:
    Exploring Race, Ethnicity, and Class.* Volume 6. Thousand Oaks, CA: Sage
    Publications, Inc.
Monteiro, Kenneth P. (Ed.). 1996. *Ethnicity and Psychology: African-, Asian-,
    Latino-, and Native-American Psychologies.* Revised Printing. Dubuque, IA:
    Kendall/Hunt.
Pedraza, Sylvia and Ruben Rumbaut (Eds.). 1996. *Origins and Destinies:
    Immigration, Race and Ethnicity in America.* Belmont, CA: Wadsworth.

CASE STUDY REFERENCES

CASE STUDY #1:
"A Love Story," by Kathy Scully Davis, in Susan Wadia-Ells and Nancy Mairs
    (Eds.), 1995, *The Adoption Reader: Birth Mothers, Adoptive Mothers, and
    Adoptive Daughters Tell Their Stories.* Seattle, WA: Seal Press; Emeryville,
    CA: Publishers Group West.
CASE STUDY #2:
"Getting Off on Feminism," by Jason Schultz, in Rebecca Walker (Ed.), 1995,
    To Be Real: Telling the Truth and Changing the Face of Feminism. New York:
    Anchor Books.
CASE STUDY #3:
"The Tale of City Pride," by William Kowinski, 1993, *Smithsonian* 24(7),
    pp. 118–132.
CASE STUDY #4:
"Punishing Institutions: The Story of Catherine (Cedar Woman)," narrated by
    Luana Ross, in Susan Lobo and Steve Talbot (Eds.), 1998, *Native American
    Voices: A Reader.* New York: Longman.
CASE STUDY #5:
"The Girl Who Wouldn't Sing," by Kit Yuen Quan, in Gloria Anzaldua (Ed.),
    1990, *Making Face, Making Soul, Haciendo Caras: Creative and Critical
    Perspectives by Feminists of Color.* San Francisco, CA: Aunt Lute Foundation
    Books.
CASE STUDY #6:
"Man Child: A Black Lesbian Feminist's Response," by Audre Lorde, 1979,
    Conditions 4, pp. 30–36.
CASE STUDY #7:
" 'White Trash' and Female in a Southern Community," by James T. Sears,
    1991, *Growing up Gay in the South: Race, Gender, and Journeys of the Spirit.*
    New York: Harrington Park Press.
CASE STUDY #8:
"The Valenzuela Family," excerpt from Leo R. Chavez, 1992, *Shadowed Lives:
    Undocumented Immigrants in American Society.* Fort Worth, TX: Harcourt
    Brace.

A Love Story[1]

Kathy Scully Davis

The fragrant lilac hedge was several feet higher than our heads as we walked around the corner of Victoria and Portland streets on that precious Mother's Day. I was about to meet my first-born child, a daughter I'd given birth to twenty-three years before.

With me were my sister and soulmate, Mary Theresa, with whom I had marked this child's birthday every April, and my sixteen-year-old daughter, Tara, a dark-haired, dark-eyed clone of Mary. I, with my bright-red hair, was the odd one out of this trio.

Tara was crabby. That morning she'd brought me the newspaper and tea, but had snarled at the cat and seemed annoyed at life in general. I had said to her, "Honey, you're the one in this group who understands the concept of the loaves and the fishes. You know I won't take any love away from you to give to someone else. I'll just manufacture more. That's what moms do."

Tara, with sixteen years of practice in identifying and articulating an emotion the instant she has it, had answered with a dark frown, "I know that. But if you manufacture more love, I want it."

As the three of us rounded the corner onto Portland, I glanced at the three-story wedgwood-blue Victorian house that had been my first-born's adoptive home until her departure for graduate school. White trim and gables framed the stained glass windows, and predictably, the three-sided porch contained a porch swing. This was unquestionably the house of my own dreams, and certainly the perfect house for raising a family, this child of mine along with four siblings and three foster children. This blue heaven advertised "home."

My twenty-three-year-old daughter inside that blue Victorian had been one of the world's more wanted children. Her biological father, Angelo, had loved me more devotedly than anyone before, or possibly since. After only three months of dating, he'd given me an engagement and wedding ring set and asked me to marry him. He was quiet, gentle, unafraid to show his feelings and not ashamed to cry. In this land of stoic, unreadable Scandinavians, those were refreshing qualities. He was also never-married, Catholic and an ex-marine, credentials highly valued by suburban Catholic parents such as mine in the early 1960s.

But he was Mexican. To my folks, a "mixed marriage" meant marrying "out of the church." To marry out of one's race was simply unthinkable. It

[1]Kathy Scully Davis, "A Love Story" from Susan Wadia-Ells and Nancy Mairs (eds.), *The Adoption Reader: Birth Mothers, Adoptive Mothers, and Adoptive Daughters Tell Their Stories* (Seattle, Wash.: Seal Press, 1995), pp. 18-26 [with cuts]. Reprinted with the permission of Seal Press.

wasn't just the church, or my family. It was part of the mores of the times. The unwritten rule was to "stick with your own kind" and offer your counterpart virtue and inexperience at the altar. Many of us didn't meet that requirement, but the standard held.

Angelo and I were sexually active: already guilt-ridden over that "transgression," I did not want to compound it by adding the immorality of birth control. I was evidently still striving for the ideal. Though Angelo was also Catholic, he did not understand how making love could be a sin.

We knew I was pregnant before I missed the first period, and intuitively, so did my mother. I was twenty-one years old, certainly not a child, and the logical action would have been to marry the father of my baby since I was already wearing his engagement ring. But I was scared, ashamed and in a serious battle with my lifelong demon, depression. Angelo, on the other hand, was overjoyed and solicitous to my every need. He was ready to plan a wedding and shop for a place to live.

I told my mother I thought I "had to get married," a quaint euphemism of the time that would mean little to a young woman today. In 1962, there were limited phrases and concepts to describe an "indelicate situation." Mom was concerned and caring but uncertain that Angelo was the man for me because I'd spent years in a relationship with my high-school sweetheart and only four months with Angelo. Mom said I didn't "have" to marry him. She'd said we'd work it out. What she didn't say—what didn't have to be said—was that if I did not marry my baby's father, the child would automatically be placed for adoption. There were only two choices: I could marry and keep the child, or I could remain unmarried and give up the baby for adoption, a baby that would be considered of "mixed-race." Finding an adoptive home for my baby might be problematic, even impossible. I agonized over the decision. I was sick more than I was well. I hardly knew this man. There was still a spot in my heart for my high-school sweetheart. Marriage was unquestionably "forever." If I married Angelo, would the marriage work, given my reservations and the cultural gap? His mother grew her own chilis!! I didn't even know what a chili was! I had been raised on potatoes, for heaven's sake! Would our families reject each other? Would they reject the baby? What if we married and the marriage didn't work? Divorce was not a possibility. And even in the remote chance of a divorce, the child would not have two parents: the whole reason for placing the child for adoption would be to ensure a "two-parent family," and of course, all the "advantages."

The pressure from my family to not marry Angelo and place the baby was intense; to them, marrying this man was out of the question. Even as I was succumbing to the pressure from my family, this man held to his adamant belief that we could overcome obstacles. But, he was one person, and my family was barraging me from all sides. It took until I was halfway through the pregnancy, but I decided against the marriage.

Angelo's very large extended family was enraged. Angelo had no clear idea why, if I wasn't going to keep the child, I wouldn't let him keep it. Who ever heard of giving away babies? In the Mexican community there is *always* a place for a baby. Where did babies go who were given away? To an orphanage? He was incredulous at the thought. Everyone in his family, especially his mother, would take care of the child. He simply could not comprehend my "logic."

So I sent long, tedious letters of explanation to him about the Natural Order of Things, having no idea whatsoever that it might not be a universal order, that it might have been true for only a small, white, suburban, notoriously unbending group of people. We were under the impression that a child should have two parents, a mother and a father. At age twenty-one, I had never heard of keeping a child without being married. Only widows did that.

My painful decision was made. My baby would have two parents. Two adoptive parents. I was sent away, of course. A pregnant daughter wasn't allowed to stay at home, even to serve as an example to other children in the household. My pregnancy, like millions of others before mine, was to be a secret. I was supposed to be sorely ashamed. I was a failure at the only thing that mattered: being a good girl.

The strangers who gave me a home that bitterly cold winter did not at any time refer to the pregnancy. I, however, was consumed by it. When I was bathing, I would watch my stomach as it moved above the bubbles. I was so in love with the little legs and arms and feet. If this baby was a girl, could I go through with the adoption? Maybe not. Perhaps I shouldn't know if it was a girl or a boy. Boys need dads. I could probably surrender a boy. But a girl? Maybe I could raise a daughter myself. Then, one day, I suddenly found myself in hard, heavy labor.

I had made several requests of the doctor and the social worker: Please render me completely unconscious. Don't let me hear the baby cry, and don't tell me anything, particularly the baby's sex. I wanted a guarantee of instant placement into the adoptive home, and that only the adoptive parents would be allowed to name the child. In my soul I thought she was a girl and had named her Theresa, after my sister. The doctor honored my requests. The agency staff honored nothing. They told me I had given birth to a daughter, and they named her.

As my sister, my young daughter and I approached the steps of the blue Victorian house, I had to instruct myself to exhale. I was a walking bundle of nerve endings. I stepped up first. Behind me, Tara, knowing from photos her new sister would be dark-haired, said to my sister, "Let's let her guess which of you is the real mom!"

The door swung open, and one of the world's most remarkable adoptive mothers threw both arms wide and said, "Welcome to our home!" I fell into her open arms.

Pat has evidently always been remarkable. She had been a public health nurse when she married and began her family. But after giving birth to two children, she was unable to carry any other pregnancies to term, a source of extreme disappointment to her, as a large family had been her lifelong dream.

Aware of all the unwanted pregnancies, then as now, Pat wept over the irony that she and her husband wanted a large family and shared a lifestyle that could accommodate one, yet were unable to have more children. Finally, because she is a practical, sensible woman, she went to Catholic Charities to apply for adoption.

Susan was the family's first adopted child. Of partially Mexican descent, she had been placed with them some months before my baby was born. The adoption laws, in the state, at that time, stated that an adoption in a family had to be final before another could be begun. Though Pat and her husband had spoken for my baby, Susan's adoption wouldn't be final for several months; consequently, my newborn was placed in a foster home. Pat pleaded with the agency to allow her to name and baptize the baby, unaware that I had also insisted on this, but because of the archaic closed adoption laws of the time, she wasn't even allowed to see or hold her.

Pat brought my baby to her home in November and shortly thereafter took her to the cathedral where she was baptized Mary Alice. Entries into Mary's baby book characterize her as "sweet, placid, maybe lazy, but with a bit of a temper." She was exceptionally beautiful, with larger-than-life brown eyes. She was good-natured and easy to raise. Pat and her husband adopted one more child after Mary, a son of Spanish descent whom they named Karl.

At that time in her life, Pat's husband began to be absent from home more and more. She could see the clear possibility of being alone with five children, so she went back to school for her master's degree in nursing.

Eventually, Pat and her husband divorced and she entered her "hungry years." On the other side of town, I, who had married and divorced my high-school sweetheart, was walking the same austere path with my two other children. Both Pat and I were extending the milk by adding powdered milk, and when there was no milk, putting water in the cereal. We managed, as poor women have always done, and somehow the kids did not feel deprived.

Pat told me later she often thought how ironic it was that three women had given their children to her, presumably so those children would have a good home with two parents. In fact, all five children were living in a single-parent home. She never had a minute of doubt she could handle the situation, yet she was glad the birth mothers didn't know what had happened to their babies. Each year when the adoptive children celebrated their birthdays, Pat reminded each of them that another mother out there somewhere was also remembering the day.

Pat managed the three-story house, grew and maintained a large garden and participated in parental activities at school while attending graduate school full time. She also began dating the man the children called "Mr. B."

I stepped forward and wrapped my arms around this woman, and she held me for a long moment. This was my daughter's mother. We whispered, "Thank you, thank you," to each other. Then, as now, I could not love her more than if she were my own sister.

Pat released me and introduced her daughter Jody, standing next to her. Petite and poised, she seemed to be loving this. Tara, behind me, was so agitated that she was oscillating. Since her brother had gone to live with his father, Tara had become accustomed to being an only child. Though she had known of her sister's existence for years, the reality that Mary Alice and possibly the rest of her family were to become a part of our lives was a definite cloud on Tara's horizon. Jody, however, was clearly curious and glad to meet us.

I looked into the shadows of the door and my eyes came to rest on Louie ("Mr. B"), Pat's second husband. A large, tall man, he nearly filled the doorway. Louie had married Pat after her divorce and his first wife's grueling death, and when Mary was twelve, had adopted all five of Pat's kids, "just in time for braces and college." Subsequently, Pat and Louie took in three foster children and offered their home to numerous others.

Louie had agreed to send Mary a ticket home from graduate school for this meeting, but his heart was clearly not in it. He was visibly apprehensive and his light blue eyes were misting over.

. . .

Likely Louie was feeling somewhat as Tara felt, that there was a new person here who was going to change the configuration, and there was no way to control it. Tara had said earlier, "This Mary is no one in particular to me. She's just another person in the universe." Underneath that bravado was terror. And there I was, another person in Louie's universe. Unknown quantities. The middle-aged man, and my sixteen-year-old, shared an uncertainty bordering on panic. The grown man and the teenager were failing to do what they both usually relied on under pressure: Keep it light, keep everyone laughing.

. . .

"Come on, Mary," Pat said into the shaded room, "Stop hiding!" The rest of the family was stacking up behind Louie. Mary came around from behind Louie, timidly, hesitantly smiling, but anxious. She was flanked by her primary support system, her entire family. I could see she was much more beautiful than the pictures she had sent me. Somewhat over five feet tall, round and quite dark-complected, she had a crop of thick, dark, wavy hair and huge dark eyes. Those were my teeth in her smile, and they were translucent.

The look on her face was a combination of curiosity and stage fright. It was as if she were thinking, "How did this happen? I was just going along living my life, being totally content with my existing family. I wasn't even all that curious, not like Susan was curious, about my biological mother, and now here she is on my doorstep. I feel nauseous. How do we act? What do we do? What if I don't like her? What if she doesn't like me? What if I throw up in her face? Maybe I could cancel this whole deal. Maybe I could wish myself to disappear. What if there had been open adoption when I was born? I'd have had to contend with this total stranger all this time. She is no one to me anyway, just another person in the universe."

Her initial letter to me the previous January had been the very letter that every woman who has given up her child wants to receive. She had told me that she'd had a wonderful life, that she'd been educated at St. Catherine's College, where she had majored in Spanish. She'd been to Mexico and to Spain. She had the greatest parents anyone could ever ask for, and she had said, "Thank you for letting me have this kind of life." The letter went on to say she couldn't imagine any other kind of life, but that she was a little curious: Did she have any birth brothers or sisters? Why was she finding white hairs in her head at twenty-three? Did anyone else have a weight problem?

She had assumed she wasn't wanted at the time of her birth—she told me later that that is a common assumption for adopted kids. But she had a rich life, a wonderful mom and an adoring grandmother. She didn't have any need for another mother-figure. Plus she had this great dad who was threatened by this bio-woman, and nothing on earth was worth making him this nervous. What else could she want? So why was she standing here looking at a total stranger who didn't really have all that much connection to her life? Someone who *gave her away?* As difficult as my decision was to place her for adoption, her decision to meet me was equally difficult, and written all over her face.

I was riveted to the ground. This was a fully grown woman of breathtaking physical beauty and with the sweetest smile on earth, and she was stepping up to me in stop-motion.

She came within arm's range. I could hardly move. As most mothers do at the moment of birth, I touched her face, her hair, put my hands on her shoulders for the first time and fell instantly and completely in love with her. I said, "You're beautiful." I touched her again, and she continued her dazzling smile. I said, "I never even touched you," and the realization struck. This is my daughter as much as if I'd been there for the first step, the first lost tooth, the first period. This priceless child of God, with her mom behind me and her dad in front of me, was my daughter. A sacred moment, as the moment of birth always is.

We hugged softly. Then tightly. She scrutinized me, and then Tara. Finally she said to us both, "Well, I guess the weight problem doesn't come from you!" But then my bodacious sister Mary Theresa stepped up to her, and she said, "Well, maybe."

Suddenly there was chaos. Everyone was being introduced to everyone else, her brothers and sisters, and her two gorgeous nephews. Louie was offering coffee, mimosa, jokes that spoke of relief and joy, jokes for which the kids assured him he needed to get "some new lines." It was noisy and confusing.

Mary Alice asked me if I would like to tour the blue Victorian. So she walked us, her biological mother and aunt and half-sister, through her childhood in that house. She was soft and gentle, poised and sweet beyond words. Despite the shattering intensity of the hour, she maintained a calm demeanor.

I felt a quarter-century of the shackles of agnosticism release in my soul. Surely, this is blessing. This is grace. This is reconciliation. The cultural sanctions were dumb, the laws of the church and the state were cruel. Maybe closed adoption is unhealthy, but this much I knew that day, and I know it as I write: That woman/child/baby belonged to Pat and Louie, to that house, to that life. It was exactly as it was meant to be. I had served as a surrogate mother for Pat: This child was meant to be with them. I don't understand it, or why it had to be so stupidly painful, but it was right. I felt surrounded by spirit. It was a consecrated moment. Resenting the rules and balking at fate the whole way, nevertheless, I had done something absolutely wonderful.

We sat down for brunch in the elegant dining room. Louie was obviously overcome with emotion yet not prepared to cry in front of all of us: He gave grace and we began to eat and to become acquainted. Tara, awed by the house and the wonderful mom and dad, to say nothing of Mary's beautiful younger brother, Karl, wondered aloud if it was too late for her to be adopted by the family! (She liked not being related to Karl, however!) I turned to my new daughter and gave her the engagement ring from her biological father that I'd worn when she was born and had worn as a pinky ring since.

Mary now wears that ring as a wedding ring since her marriage. Her family and I have an ongoing relationship, one that allowed me to attend her wedding, fulfilling a lifelong dream for me. I was inadvertently the main mother of the bride that day because Pat was in the hospital for emergency surgery.

Mary and her husband Mark and Pat and Louie have visited my parents in Arizona. My mother wept openly, and I heard her say for the first time, "We were never really sure we did the right thing." (*Now* she tells me! Go figure!) My family and I can now see what Mary Alice has always known: Pat and Louie and Mary, as well as the rest of the houseful of children and foster-children, belonged together.

Once Pat and I packed suitcases and drove up to Fargo, where Mary was beginning her career. She introduced us as "my moms." We are family. Since we've met, Pat has never referred to Mary Alice as other than "our daughter."

Now all eight children are gone from the blue Victorian, and the house has recently been sold. From a photograph of the house, I will cross-stitch a sampler for Mary. And Pat and Louie will be moving to my neighborhood, where we will continue our rich friendship, dear love for each other and staggering respect.

Sometimes, at odd moments, my heart becomes very full. There are so many adoptive parents aching for a child, and so many unplanned children, often born to women who have few resources. Currently, pregnant women experience extreme societal pressure to keep their babies, regardless of what is in the best interest of those babies. And there are laws that continue to pull babies from adoptive homes and put them back with biological parents, also despite what is best for the child. Babies are treated as property. Many children are not as lucky as my Mary Alice.

I am older now and wiser, and I know something I didn't know as a young woman: Love isn't enough. Love does *not* conquer all. Often, the greatest act of love is to give a child loving parents *and* some opportunities. Personal experience in our now blended family shows me clearly that loving parents don't need to be related by blood to their children. We are all children of God, or the universe, or life. Each new baby deserves the best home, and sometimes that isn't the home of the biological parents.

Kahlil Gibran says, "Your children are not your children. They are the sons and daughters of Life's longing for itself." He also says, "All you have shall some day be given."

And I reply: *Everything we give comes back to us, a thousandfold.*

QUESTIONS FOR DISCUSSION AND ANALYSIS

Historically and Geographically/Globally Contextual

1. Trace the historical definitions of *family* throughout this story. Does family mean something different as Kathy writes than it did in 1962? Or does her definition of family stay the same throughout the narrative?
2. In this story, biological mothers seem much more important to children than biological fathers. How are parents of different genders defined and discussed differently? How have ideas about motherhood and fatherhood developed and changed over the time frame in this story?
3. If Kathy turned 21 in 2000, how might her decisions have been different? Would she have had sex before marriage? Would she have used contraception? If she had become pregnant, would she have given up her child? Would she have been sent away to live with strangers while she was pregnant? Would she have married Angelo? Would Angelo have proposed?
4. How might Kathy's views have changed by living through historical social movements (such as Civil Rights, Women's, Gay and Lesbian, etc.) after she gave Mary Alice up for adoption?
5. Shifts in adoption laws in recent years have allowed birth mothers and their adopted children to stay in touch. "Open" adoptions can now take place, yet when Mary Alice was born most adoptions were "closed." How might Mary Alice's life have been different if her adoption had been open?
6. If Kathy had not lived in a small, White suburban community but instead lived in a large, urban racially-mixed city, how might her choices and decisions have been influenced?

Socially Constructed

7. Discuss the cultural differences in keeping and raising children between working-class Mexican communities and White, middle-class suburban communities. What is different and what is similar? Why was it so strange for Angelo to think of giving away a child, yet for Kathy to think it fairly normal?

8. Kathy concludes, "Love does *not* conquer all. Often, the greatest act of love is to give a child loving parents *and* some opportunities." In addition, she states that "the whole reason for placing the child for adoption would be to ensure a 'two-parent family,' and of course, all the 'advantages.'" What does she mean? Why is a two-parent family assumed to be better for the child? How has this assumption worked to reinforce race, class, gender and sexuality hierachies?

9. Like the stories of Theo and Lynn Johnson (Weber 2001), Kathy also refers to her dreams. What kinds of dreams does she have, and how do they illustrate hierarchies of race, class, gender, and sexuality? What do her dreams have to do with oppression and privilege?

10. Why was Kathy sent away by her parents during her pregnancy? How is single motherhood socially constructed? Does the construction vary for White women and women of color? Middle–class and poor women?

11. Why was Kathy worried that her baby might not be adopted because it was "mixed race"? How are interracial families socially constructed? Does this construction support or challenge racial ethnic divisions?

12. Imagine that Kathy was Mexican American and Angelo was White. How would the story change?

13. This story presents a happy picture of a reunion and the development of a deep friendship between biological and adoptive families. Do you think this is a complete portrayal of these individuals' lives? Whose feelings are not discussed? What aspects of these families' lives are disregarded? How might the story change if someone else were narrating it?

Power Relationships

14. What kind of power has Kathy had over her own decisions throughout her life? Who else has had power over Kathy's life? In what ways do Pat and Mary Alice both have and lack the power to control their lives?

15. How are power relationships of race, class, gender, and sexuality expressed in the relationships of Angelo, Kathy, Pat, and Mary Alice to one another?

16. What institutional patterns of family are reinforced in this story? What race, class, gender, and sexuality groups benefit? Are dominant patterns of race, class, gender, and sexuality challenged in the story? How?

17. In what ways does Kathy, Mary Alice, and Pat's success challenge power structures of race, class, gender, and sexuality? In what ways does their success reinforce dominant power relations?

18. Does Kathy ever resist power structures in making her decision to give up her child? Is she resisting oppression at the end of this vignette? How?

19. How is sexuality discussed in this story? How does Kathy talk about her experience with premarital sex and contraception? Is heterosexuality upheld or challenged in this story?

20. If Pat had been a lesbian, how might her story have been different? Would she have been allowed to adopt children and be a foster mother? What types of people and families are allowed and are likely to adopt a child? Why? How does the institution of adoption support race, class, gender, and sexuality hierarchies?

Macro/Social Structural and Micro/Social Psychological Levels

21. How has the institution of religion affected Kathy's and Mary Alice's lives? How does each person in turn use religion to explain his or her life? Are race, class, gender, and sexuality hierarchies reinforced or challenged by the religious beliefs of the people in this story?
22. Is Kathy in favor of adoption? Do structural and/or individual factors shape her opinion? What does Kathy suggest about the importance of parents' biological ties to children?
23. Why are Angelo's (and his family's) wishes to keep his child never granted? Why did the biological mother and her family get to make the decision for adoption and disregard Angelo's position? How does Kathy work to define Angelo (and his family) as "Other"?
24. What institutional arrangements have privileged Kathy? Is Kathy aware of the privileges she has?
25. What are the conditions that enable Kathy and Mary Alice to reunite? What are the conditions that do not allow the same for Angelo and Mary Alice?
26. If Mary Alice had been African American, would she have been as likely to be adopted? What race are the majority of children who are adopted? What race/ethnicities are the majority of children in foster care—those who do not get adopted? Why?
27. Mary Alice's biological parents are Mexican and White. She was adopted and raised by a White woman, with three adopted siblings of Mexican and Spanish descent. How might this affect her racial ethnic identity? Do you think she identifies as White, Mexican, or both? How might this change over time? What types of privilege and oppression might she experience because of her racial ethnic identity?

Simultaneously Expressed

28. How have gender, sexuality, race, and class simultaneously affected Kathy's personal choices in motherhood?
29. Could we say that Kathy is oppressed or privileged or both by her race, class, gender, sexuality, and religion? Do you think Kathy would consider herself privileged or oppressed or both? What about Angelo?
30. Kathy says that she failed the only thing that mattered: being a "good girl." How can we discuss this statement in terms of structures of gender and sexuality oppression?

31. Although never explicitly stated, what would you surmise about Pat's and Louie's class, race, religion, and sexuality? Why does this matter?
32. Was/Is Kathy acting in a racist manner in her decision not to marry Angelo and to give Mary Alice up for adoption? Why or why not? Were her parents acting in a racist and/or classist manner? How do race, class, gender, and sexuality all influence the parents' decision?

Implications for Social Action and Social Justice

33. In some ways, Kathy is trying to redefine herself and her choices through this narration. Does this process of self-definition point to ways we can transform race, class, gender, and sexuality hierarchies?
34. What implications does the ending of this story have for adoption policies? How might this narrative be employed to change adoption policies?
35. In what ways did the dominant ideology and gendered construction of family work in this case to inhibit and restrict rather than support families? How could those processes be changed?

REFERENCES

Carp, E. Wayne. 1998. *Family Matters: Secrecy and Disclosure in the History of Adoption.* Cambridge, MA: Harvard University Press.

Coontz, Stephanie (Ed.). 1999. *American Families: A Multicultural Reader.* New York: Routledge.

_____ 1992. *The Way We Never Were: American Families and the Nostalgia Trap.* New York: Basic Books.

_____ 1997. *The Way We Really Are: Coming to Terms with America's Changing Families.* New York: Basic Books.

Glenn, Evelyn Nakano and Grace Chang (Eds.). 1994. *Mothering: Ideology, Experience and Agency.* New York: Routledge.

Grotevant, Harold D. 1998. *Openness in Adoption: Exploring Family Connections.* Thousand Oaks, CA: Sage Publications, Inc.

Solinger, Rickie. 1992. *Wake Up Little Suzie: Single Pregnancy and Race Before Roe vs. Wade.* New York: Routledge.

Triseliotis, John, Joan Shireman, and Marion Hundleby. 1997. *Adoption: Theory, Policy and Practice.* London: Cassell.

Wadia-Ells, Susan and Nancy Mairs (Eds.). 1995. *The Adoption Reader: Birth Mothers, Adoptive Mothers, and Adoptive Daughters Tell Their Stories.* Seattle, WA: Seal Press; Emeryville, CA: Publishers Group West.

CASE STUDY 2

Getting Off on Feminism[1]

Jason Schultz

When it comes to smashing a paradigm, pleasure is not the most important thing. It is the only thing. —Gary Wolf, Wired *Magazine*

minutes after my best friend told me he was getting married, I casually offered to throw a bachelor party in his honor. Even though such parties are notorious for their degradation of women, I didn't think this party would be much of a problem. Both the bride and groom considered themselves feminists, and I figured that most of the men attending would agree that sexism had no place in the celebration of this union. In fact, I thought the bachelor party would be a great opportunity to get a group of men together for a social event that didn't degenerate into the typical anti-women, homophobic male-bonding thing. Still, ending one of the most sexist traditions in history—even for one night—was a lot tougher than I envisioned.

I have to admit that I'm not a *complete* iconoclast: I wanted to make the party a success by including at least some of the usual elements, such as good food and drink, great music, and cool things to do. At the same time, I was determined not to fall prey to traditional sexist party gimmicks such as prostitutes, strippers jumping out of cakes, or straight porn. But after nixing all the traditional lore, even *I* thought it sounded boring. What were we going to do except sit around and think about women?

"What about a belly dancer?" one of the ushers suggested when I confided my concerns to him. "That's not as bad as a stripper." I sighed. This was supposed to be an occasion for the groom and his male friends to get together, celebrate the upcoming marriage, and affirm their friendship and connection with each other as men. "What the fuck does hiring a female sex worker have to do with any of that?" I shouted into the phone. I quickly regained my calm, but his suggestion still stung. We had to find some other way.

I wanted my party to be as "sexy" as the rest of them, but I had no idea how to do that in the absence of female sex workers. There was no powerful alternative image in our culture from which I could draw. I thought about renting some gay porn, or making it a cross-dressing party, but many of the guests were conservative, and I didn't want to scare anyone off. Besides, what would it say about a bunch of straight men if all we could do to be sexy was act queer for a night?

Over coffee on a Sunday morning, I asked some of the other guys what they thought was so "sexy" about having a stripper at a bachelor party.

[1]Jason Schultz, "Getting Off on Feminism" from Rebecca Edby Walker (ed.), *To Be Real: Telling the Truth and Changing the Face of Feminism* (New York: Anchor Books, 1995). Copyright © 1995 by Jason Schultz. Reprinted with the permission of the author. The author can be contacted at jschultz@alumni.Duke.edu.

21

"Well," David said, "it's just a gag. It's something kinda funny and sexy at the same time."

"Yeah," A.J. agreed. "It's not all that serious, but it's something special to do that makes the party cool."

"But *why* is it sexy and funny?" I asked. "Why can't we, as a bunch of guys, be sexy and funny ourselves?"

" 'Cause it's easier to be a guy with other guys when there's a chick around. It gives you all something in common to relate to."

"Hmm. I think I know what you mean," I said. "When I see a stripper, I get turned on, but not in the same way I would if I was with a lover. It's more like going to a show or watching a flick together. It's enjoyable, stimulating, but it's not overwhelming or intimate in the same way that sex is. Having the stripper provides a common emotional context for us to feel turned on. But we don't have to do anything about it like we would if we were with a girlfriend, right?"

"Well, my girlfriend would kill me if she saw me checking out this stripper," Greg replied. "But because it's kind of a male-bonding thing, it's not as threatening to our relationship. It's not because it's the stripper over her, it's because it's just us guys hanging out. It doesn't go past that."

Others agreed. "Yeah. You get turned on, but not in a serious way. It makes you feel sexy and sexual, and you can enjoy feeling that way with your friends. Otherwise, a lot of times, just hanging out with the guys is pretty boring. Especially at a bachelor party. I mean, that's the whole point, isn't it—to celebrate the fact that we're bachelors, and he"—referring to Robert, the groom—"isn't!"

Through these conversations, I realized that having a female sex worker at the party would give the men permission to connect with one another without becoming vulnerable. When men discuss sex in terms of actions—who they "did," and how and where they did it—they can gain recognition and validation of their sexuality from other men without having to expose their *feelings* about sex.

"What other kinds of things make you feel sexy like the stripper does?" I asked several of the guys.

"Watching porn sometimes, or a sexy movie."

A.J. said, "Just getting a look from a girl at a club. I mean, she doesn't even have to talk to you, but you still feel sexy and you can still hang out with your friends."

Greg added, "Sometimes just knowing that my girlfriend thinks I'm sexy, and then talking about her with friends, makes me feel like I'm the man. Or I'll hear some other guy talk about his girlfriend in a way that reminds me of mine, and I'll still get that same feeling. But that doesn't happen very often, and usually only when talking with one other guy.

This gave me an idea. "I've noticed that same thing, both here and at school with my other close guy friends. Why doesn't it happen with a bunch of guys, say at a party?"

"I don't know. It's hard to share a lot of personal stuff with guys," said Adam, "especially about someone you're seeing, if you don't feel comfortable.

Well, not comfortable, because I know most of the guys who'll be at the party, but it's more like I don't want them to hassle me, or I might say something that freaks them out."

"Or you're just used to guys talking shit about girls," someone else added. "Like at a party or hanging out together. They rag on them, or pick out who's the cutest or who wants to do who. That's not the same thing as really talking about what makes you feel sexy."

"Hmm," I said. "So it's kind of like if I were to say that I liked to be tied down to the bed, no one would take me seriously. You guys would probably crack up laughing, make a joke or two, but I'd never expect you to actually join in and talk about being tied up in a serious way. It certainly wouldn't feel 'sexy,' would it? At least not as much as the stripper."

"Exactly. You talking about being tied down here is fine, 'cause we're into the subject of sex on a serious kick and all. But at a party, people are bullshitting each other and gabbing, and horsing around. The last thing most of us want is to trip over someone's personal taste or start thinking someone's a little queer."

"You mean queer as in homosexual?" I asked.

"Well, not really, 'cause I think everyone here is straight. But more of queer in the sense of perverted or different. I mean, you grow up in high school thinking that all guys are basically the same. You all want the same thing from girls in the same way. And when someone like you says you like to be tied down, it's kinda weird—almost like a challenge. It makes me have to respond in a way that either shows me agreeing that I also like to be tied down or not. And if someone's a typical guy and he says that, it makes you think he's different—not the same guy you knew in high school. And if he's not the same guy, then it challenges you to relate to him on a different level."

"Yeah, I guess in some ways it's like relating to someone who's gay," Greg said. "He can be cool and all, and you can get along totally great. But there's this barrier that's hard to cross over. It kinda keeps you apart. And that's not what you want to feel toward your friends, especially at a party like this one, where you're all coming together to chill."

As the bachelor party approached, I found myself wondering whether my friends and I could "come together to chill"—and affirm our status as sexual straight men—without buying into homophobic or sexist expressions. At the same time, I was doing a lot of soul-searching on how we could challenge the dominant culture's vision of male heterosexuality, not only by deciding against having a stripper at our party, but also by examining and redefining our own relationships with women.

. . .

Breaking the silence   Not becoming a sitting target to have *my* manhood shot down was high on my mind when the evening of my best friend's bachelor party finally arrived. But I was determined not to be silent about how I felt about the party and about new visions for straight men within our society.

We decided to throw the party two nights before the wedding. We all gathered at my house, each of us bringing a present to add to the night's activities. After all the men had arrived, we began cooking dinner, breaking open beer and champagne, and catching up on where we had left off since we last saw each other.

During the evening, we continued to talk off and on about why we didn't have a stripper or prostitute for the party. After several rounds of margaritas and a few hands of poker, tension started to build around the direction I was pushing the conversation.

"So what don't you like about strippers?" David asked me.

This was an interesting question. I was surprised not only by the guts of David to ask it, but also by my own mixed feelings in coming up with an answer. "It's not that I don't like being excited, or turned on, per se," I responded. "In fact, to be honest, watching a female stripper is an exciting and erotic experience for me. But at the same time, it's a very uncomfortable one. I get a sense when I watch her that I'm participating in a misuse of pleasure, if that makes sense."

I looked around at my friends. I couldn't tell whether the confused looks on their faces were due to the alcohol, the poker game, or my answer, so I continued. "Ideally, I would love to sit back and enjoy watching someone express herself sexually through dance, seduction, flirtation—all the positive elements I associate with stripping," I said. "But at the same time, because so many strippers are poor and forced to perform in order to survive economically, I feel like the turn-on I get is false. I feel like I get off easy, sitting back as the man, paying for the show. No one ever expects me to get up on stage.

"And in that way, it's selling myself short sexually. It's not only saying very little about the sexual worth of the woman on stage, but the sexual worth of me as the viewer as well. By *only* being a viewer—just getting off as a member of the audience—the striptease becomes a very limiting thing, an imbalanced dynamic. If the purpose is for me to feel sexy and excited, but not to act on those feelings, I'd rather find a more honest and direct way to do it. So personally, while I would enjoy watching a stripper on one level, the real issues of economics, the treatment of women, and the limitation of my own sexual personae push me to reject the whole stripper thing in favor of something else."

"But what else do you do to feel sexy?" A.J. asked.

"That's a tough question," I said. "Feeling sexy often depends on the way other people act toward you. For me, right now, you guys are a huge way for me to feel sexy. [Some of the men cringe.] I'm not saying that we have to challenge our sexual identities, although that's one way. But we can cut through a lot of this locker-room macho crap and start talking with each other about how we feel sexually, what we think, what we like, etc. Watching the stripper makes us feel sexy because we get turned on through the dynamic between her performance and our voyeurism. We can find that same erotic connection with each other by re-creating that context between us. In such a case, we're still heterosexual—we're no more having sex with each other than we are with the stripper. But we're not relying on the imbalanced dynamic of sex work to feel pleasure as straight men."

. . .

The guys were silent for a few seconds, but soon afterwards, the ice seemed to break.

. . .

They agreed that, as heterosexual men, we should be able to share with each other what we find exciting and shouldn't *need* a female stripper to feel sexy. In some ways it may have been the desire to define their own sexuality that changed their minds; in others it may have been a traditionally masculine desire to reject any dependency on women. In any case, other men began to speak of their own experiences with pleasure and desire, and we continued to talk throughout the night, exploring the joys of hot sex, one-night stands, and even our preferences for certain brands of condoms. We discussed the ups and down of monogamy versus "open" dating and the pains of long-distance relationships.

Some men continued to talk openly about their desire for straight pornography or women who fit the traditional stereotype of femininity. But others contradicted this, expressing their wish to move beyond that image of women in their lives. The wedding, which started out as the circumstance for our gathering, soon fell into the background of our thoughts as we focused away from institutional ideas of breeder sexuality and began to find common ground through our real-life experiences and feelings as straight men. In the end, we all toasted the groom, sharing stories, jokes, and parts of our lives that many of us had never told. Most importantly, we were able to express ourselves sexually without hiding who we were from each other.

Thinking back on the party, I realized that the hard part was figuring out what we all wanted and how to construct a different way of finding that experience. The other men there wanted it just as much as I did. The problem was that we had no ideas of what a different kind of bachelor party might look like. Merely eliminating the old ways of relating (i.e., the female sex workers) left a gap, an empty space which in many ways *felt* worse than the sexist connection that existed there before; we felt passive and powerless. Yet we found a new way of interacting—one that embraced new ideas and shared the risk of experiencing them.

Was the party sexy? Did we challenge the dominance of oppressive male sexuality? Not completely, but it was a start. I doubt anyone found my party as "sexy" as traditional ones might be, but the dialogue has to start somewhere. It's going to take a while to generate the language and collective tension to balance the cultural image of heterosexual male sexuality with true sexual diversity. Still, one of my friends from high school—who's generally on the conservative end of most issues—told me as he was leaving that of all the bachelor parties he had been to, this was by far the best one. "I had a great time," he said. "Even without the stripper."

. . .

QUESTIONS FOR DISCUSSION AND ANALYSIS

Historically and Geographically/Globally Contextual

1. Jason writes of his experiences coming of age as a man in the 1990s. How might Jason's situation be different if he lived in a different time period? Could Jason have pulled off this type of bachelor party in the 1950s? Why or why not?
2. Historically, how has White, middle-class, heterosexual masculinity been socially constructed? For whom is this construction beneficial, according to Jason? Whom does it harm?
3. Jason discusses how the bride and groom self-identified as feminists and clearly espouses his own version of feminism. In this context, how would Jason define feminism? Is this definition positive or negative or both? Would Jason, the bride, and the groom have defined themselves as feminists a decade ago? In the 1970s? In the 1950s? Discuss the historically contextual nature of feminism.
4. Where did the notion of a bachelor party originate in U.S. society? What groups of men tend to participate in this ritual?

Socially Constructed

5. Despite Jason's attempts to challenge current definitions of class, gender, and sexuality, which structures of oppression are left intact and why? Does Jason challenge the institutions of heterosexuality or marriage?
6. Jason believes that men must be able to feel "sexy" at bachelor parties. What does he mean by sexy? Why do men expect to feel sexy in these situations? How does Jason challenge those expectations?
7. Much of Jason's story deals with the idea that men cannot relate to each other in a social group and that many need to have a diversion that will reduce tension in all-male gatherings. Why?
8. Do Jason and his friends show that men can be feminists too? Is their feminism different from that of their women friends?
9. In what ways does acting out their privileged position as White, heterosexual, middle-class males restrict the range of behavior available and acceptable for them? Why? How is privilege (race, class, gender, and sexuality) constructed in this story?

Power Relationships

10. What power relations do Jason and his friends reinforce in the story? In the end, do they seriously challenge the sex and gender system of inequality?
11. What does Jason mean when he suggests that the use of a stripper limits male sexuality? What does this have to do with power?

12. Do strippers have power as they work? If so, what types of power do they have? In what ways are strippers oppressed?

Macro/Social Structural and Micro/Social Psychological Levels

13. What are the institutional arrangements that allow Jason and/or the groom to begin pondering what a feminist bachelor party would look like?
14. What reasons does Jason give for not wanting to have a stripper at his best friend's bachelor party? How do these reasons relate to larger structures of oppression and privilege?
15. While it seems that this new type of bachelor party has the potential to challenge certain social hierarchies, is this new version of a bachelor party enough? How significant are Jason's efforts in the larger picture?
16. Since men ultimately have power over women in our society, what does Jason mean when he implies that men also face gender and sexuality oppression?
17. What are some of the personal consequences Jason may face when he resists gender and sexuality oppression?
18. Who are the men who seem most likely to identify as feminists today? Why?

Simultaneously Expressed

19. How does the atmosphere of a bachelor party constrain or define men's reactions to the strippers/porn movies? Is it socially acceptable for men to get aroused at a bachelor party?
20. Why are race and class never mentioned in this story? What is the significance of Jason's ignoring race and class at the same time he is discussing gender and sexuality?
21. When the night of the bachelor party arrived, why was Jason worried about having his own manhood challenged? What did he fear?
22. Why did this "new" kind of bachelor party still exclude women? What are the implications for gender relations?
23. Are bachelor parties common among African-American, Latino, Asian, and non-Christian communities? How is hegemonic White, middle-class masculinity being constructed in this story?

Implications for Social Action and Social Justice

24. In creating a new kind of bachelor party, what is Jason's goal? Does he achieve it? Who benefits from this new type of bachelor party? All men? Certain groups of men? All women? Certain groups of women?
25. If Jason's bachelor party challenges male forms of sexism, how could women challenge structures of oppression at bridal showers or bachelorette

parties? What would you do if you were a maid of honor for a wedding and had the assignment of challenging gender and sexuality hierarchies when planning one of these events? How could you resist societal definitions of women, men, marriage, and heterosexuality? What would feminist wedding rituals encompass?

26. For whom does Jason write? Who is his audience? Who can relate to this story? All men? All women? Feminists? Only certain groups of men or women?

REFERENCES

Brod, Harry and Michael Kimmel (Eds.). 1994. *Theorizing Masculinities.* Thousand Oakes, CA: Sage Publications, Inc.

Digby, Tom (Ed.). 1998. *Men Doing Feminism.* New York: Routledge.

Kimmel, Michael and Michael Messner. 2001. *Men's Lives.* 3rd Edition. Boston: Allyn and Bacon.

Levit, Nancy. 1998. *The Gender Line: Men, Women, and the Law.* New York: New York University Press.

Schact, Steven P. and Doris W. Ewing (Eds.). 1998. *Feminism and Men: Reconstructing Gender Relations.* New York: New York University Press.

Tobias, Sheila. 1997. *Faces of Feminism: An Activist's Reflections on the Women's Movement.* Boulder, CO: Westview Press.

Walker, Rebecca (Ed.). 1995. *To Be Real: Telling the Truth and Changing the Face of Feminism.* New York: Anchor Books.

CASE STUDY 3

The Tale of City Pride[1]

William Severini Kowinski

*When a Pittsburgh bakery closed its doors, unemployed workers took a big gamble—
and found a way to make their daily bread*

. . .

In March 1989 the notice simply appeared on the bulletin board near the
lunchroom door, the one they always checked for new job postings and other information. In 60 days the Braun Bakery would shut down production and close
its doors, after a hundred years of baking bread for Pittsburgh, Pennsylvania.

For Ralston Purina, the international conglomerate that now owned the
bakery, the closing was part of a national reorganization. It seemed more eco-
nomical to make its products at a few mega-plants, like one in Philadelphia,
and ship to cities like Pittsburgh.

At first, some workers, such as Wilma Harris,[2] refused to believe it. She'd
been at Braun's for 13 years and, at 43, had two grown children and two
granddaughters living with her.

A small-boned woman with a ready smile, Harris paused from her job
running the bread bagger to look around the noisy plant floor. There was
Pearl Alexandre, who came aboard the same year she did; and Chuck Geiger,
who started a year earlier. They'd be in trouble, too. But it was even worse for
the old hands who would lose out on their pensions, like Richard Sipes, a 20-
year veteran in the shipping department; Ali Deen, with 22 years; or Joe Zajac,
who'd worked his way up to production assistant superintendent over
30 years at the bakery.

Some, like Harris, were from the predominantly Black neighborhoods
near the Braun's plant, on Pittsburgh's North Side; others came from the city's
ethnic neighborhoods—Polish, Italian and so forth. They all worked hard together, and they made good bread.

Yet, except for Wilma Harris and her coworkers, the closing of this single
plant could seem like no big deal. After all, thousands of manufacturing jobs
had been lost in this region in the past decade already, so what were 110
more? And what could they do anyway? It might be a one-day Pittsburgh
story, worth a few minutes on the evening news, when the last loaf of bread
rolled out and Pittsburgh lost its last commercial bakery.

But that's not what happened.

. . .

From the first meeting at the Local 12 hall of the Bakery, Confectionery and Tobacco Workers Union, the workers spoke with sadness and anger. "This is a bakery where people worked until they died, and their sons went to work after them," said Walt Salachup, at Braun's for 21 years. "We have a lot of fathers and sons working here together," said Mike Melaragno, who had worked at Braun's since he came from Italy in 1955.

The announcement of Braun's closing also saddened and angered Pittsburgh. Even in a city used to plant closings, a shiver went down the civic spine, for Braun's was the last of the Pittsburgh bread makers, dating back to 1889. When Mike Melaragno started at Braun's in the 1950s, its octogenarian founder still occasionally came to the bakery, pulled up a chair and watched.

Mobilizing a Rescue Team   After E. R. Braun died in 1958, his company was acquired by Continental, the nation's largest bread-making company; at that time, Pittsburgh was the eighth-largest bread market in the United States. But familiar brands soon started disappearing, as other local bakeries closed and consolidated. Continental itself was swallowed up by ITT and, in 1984, was purchased by Ralston Purina. But the Braun name and original bakery plant had survived. So when the news hit of Braun's imminent closing, Pittsburgh mobilized its forces to save it. City and county politicians— even the state's senior U.S. Senator, the late John Heinz—together with the union and a number of other organizations formed a coalition to try to persuade Continental to reconsider. They came up with a $3.4 million package of tax credits, subsidies and other assistance to keep Braun's open. Meanwhile, as meetings became more frequent, the workers kept baking and delivering the bread. "Even though the people knew the plant was closing, they kept on working," says Joe Zajac, now manager of purchasing and inventory control.

. . .

Rescue efforts were futile. The plant closed on May 13, as scheduled. . . . Then the Braun's workers faced some crucial personal decisions. For many, the first and most poignant was whether to stay in Pittsburgh.

Given the choice, Pittsburghers—especially blue-collar Pittsburghers— stay put. But when the steel industry collapsed in the early 1980s, taking with it thousands of related manufacturing jobs, some 115,000 residents fled Pittsburgh and surrounding Allegheny County. It was the second-largest population loss in the country, with the city of Pittsburgh dropping from 677,000 people in 1950 to 370,000 in 1990. While there has been some growth in new high-technology and service jobs, this prosperity largely eludes workers from the old industries.

The choice for Braun's workers was made even sharper when Continental offered jobs in its huge Philadelphia bakery and a $1,500 moving allowance to any Braun's employee who would relocate.

But at that first union meeting, the Braun's workers had affirmed a fateful decision that would set the stage for everything that was to come. When 20-

year veteran Frank DeMino announced forcefully that he wasn't going to leave Pittsburgh, the other workers cheered.

"It's just someplace different," Richard Sipes explains. "I've lived in quite a few states and overseas, but there's no place like Pittsburgh. And there's no way I would leave." Eventually, only three of the Braun's employees went to Philadelphia; all were supervisors, and all came back.

There was also a strong feeling within the group to stick together. So, during the two months between the announcement and the closing, as the coalition leaders tried to keep Braun's from closing or find another buyer, some of the employees began to toss around another idea.

. . .

"We were sitting in the lunchroom and we said, why can't we get our own bakery?" Richard Sipes recalls.

They already had a strong ally. The coalition that tried to keep the Braun plant open kept working even after that effort failed. Particularly active was the Steel Valley Authority and its executive director, Tom Croft.

Pittsburgh and nearby towns were the nation's steel center for nearly a century, outproducing the rest of the world during World War II. In the mid-1980s, the fury and frustration accompanying the tearing down of these factories led to a series of angry milltown meetings. The meetings didn't save the mills but did result in an innovative state-chartered agency, the Steel Valley Authority. It was formed to encourage economic development in nine western Pennsylvania communities, including Pittsburgh. With an active staff knowledgeable in researching and putting together redevelopment deals for the industrial workers left behind, one of the SVA's tasks is to look out for troubled industries by talking with businesses and public officials. Through this "early warning network," Tom Croft heard about Braun's and joined the effort to save it.

When a core of 62 former Braun's workers decided to explore starting their own bakery, they asked him: Why couldn't we build a new plant ourselves? To someone else it might have seemed a hopeless pipe dream. But Croft, who'd created programs for dislocated workers in Seattle before coming to Pittsburgh, saw something special in the Braun's people. "I've worked with shipyard workers and steelworkers and lumber workers," he says, "and I've never seen a group as cohesive and smart and savvy and dedicated as this group."

First, Croft helped them organize a start-up committee. Joe Zajac, the only member of Braun's management to join the effort, was elected chairman. Wilma Harris was a member. One of their first tasks was to come up with a name for their prospective company. Instead of hiring an advertising or public relations firm, the workers tried to come up with a name themselves. Harris recalls asking her sister, Diane Arnett, for suggestions. "She started writing down names. Then she got some cardboard and put a black outline of the city skyline on it, and wrote the name under it: City Pride." Harris took it to the next meeting where Sam Papa, the union president, held up all the suggestions. Diane Arnett's idea won.

That summer of 1989 began with optimism and hope. Workers armed with pencils and clipboards fanned out with petitions to get grocers and potential consumers to say they'd like to buy City Pride bread. Forty grocers and more than 6,000 citizens signed. "They knew what we were going through," Chuck Geiger says. "We went to mom-and-pop stores, any place that sold bread. We stopped people on street corners. I never ran into one individual who said no. Not one."

. . .

Wilma Harris joined the others on bus trips to Harrisburg to lobby state representatives and state agencies, and went downtown to talk with city and county officials. The state came through with money for a study—if the workers would contribute 10 percent of the cost. This came out to $50 each. One of the first to put his money in was Ali Deen. "It was either go to Philadelphia or start our own bakery," he explains. "If you go someplace else you start all over again, and that's what we didn't want. For us old folks that's the bottom line."

The group's morale peaked during the Labor Day parade, which is still one of the biggest in the country. On a hot, sunny day, they marched for the first time under the banner of City Pride, sold City Pride hats and buttons, and wrapped a Volkswagen bus to make it look like a loaf of bread. "People were shouting at us, 'When are you going to open?' " Harris remembers.

Then, when a study by a food industry consultant made it clear that Braun's withdrawal meant that Pittsburgh was now the largest metropolitan area in the country without a major bread maker, City Pride hired a project manager to do a detailed feasibility study and work out a plan for getting a plant and equipment. Harris and the others were excited. Some of them were talking about being open for business in March, a year after Braun's closed.

But as autumn deepened, the project manager had bad news. "He seemed so negative," Harris recalls. In fact, his study was showing that starting a new bakery wasn't going to work. "At this juncture, the project appeared ready to die," Croft says.

But then the workers got two big breaks, at least one of which could safely be called an act of God. The first was the snowstorm in December 1989. "We didn't get too much of it here," Zajac remembers, "but it hit the outlying areas and stopped the trucks from bringing the bread in." Pittsburgh's bread was coming in from Ohio, Philadelphia and even Buffalo, and when the storm roared off Lake Erie and halted traffic on Interstate 80, there was no bread on Pittsburgh's shelves for Christmas.

Croft and the others saw the opening. "We'd been talking about how we could produce bread of high quality," he says. "But at this point we began asking, 'Do you want bread in this town or not?' " The supermarket chains started listening. Even on snowless days, their bread was anywhere from three days to a week old when it hit the shelves.

The other big break was a fellow with a suitcase, a man from California named Dan Curtis. He was asked to come to Pittsburgh by City Pride's first project manager, who wanted his findings to be reviewed by other experts. An affable, enthusiastic 36-year veteran of the bakery business, Curtis was supposed to do a quick three-day quantitative study; but as it turned out, he did much more—and stayed much longer.

. . .

On his first trip to Pittsburgh he impressed the City Pride people. On a scouting trip to local stores, Zajac watched Curtis talk to a supermarket manager known to be difficult. "He took command of that situation," says Zajac. "He's a real salesman. When I made my report at the next meeting, I said, 'I think this is the person we need to get us off the ground.' "

Curtis disagreed with the findings of the project manager. He believed that if City Pride sold itself not as a new brand but instead as the sole wholesale supplier of fresh bread to a supermarket's own label, it would start strong and grow. He also believed that the city's response was a key element.

When the City Pride workers asked Curtis to stay with the project, he said no. "I'd never been in Pittsburgh in my life; I wasn't interested in moving there. But just looking at their faces and the condition of the city, I said, 'Well, I'll give you a couple of weeks.' " Those weeks stretched into a year, and then two more years.

In March 1990, a year after the Braun's plant closed, Curtis became City Pride's project manager. After several months of flying back and forth from California, he moved into a hotel and then an apartment. His days were hectic. After a walk at 4 A.M. and church at 6, he held a half-dozen or so major meetings around the city with possible customers and backers, and often flew off to meet potential investors in other cities. "I went out on the street and knocked on a ton of doors. I know the streets of Pittsburgh very well now," Curtis says. "At first we were turned down by everybody. I kept going to a level above— in some cases I got to the very top—and just did not accept no."

Meanwhile, the 57 workers who now formed City Pride had to face making ends meet. Unemployment insurance was helping, but it wasn't enough for everyone. Some were on food stamps. Zajac was living from his savings; he needed an operation on his knees, but he put it off so he could continue to work on the project.

Pearl Alexandre followed her husband to Florida, where he had a job. Through her union, Wilma Harris got a job at Nabisco, packing chocolate chip cookies. But they still stayed with City Pride. As a committee member, Harris was responsible for calling ten or so others to remind them of the monthly meetings or to tell them what happened at the last one if they missed it. Alexandre managed to keep in touch by mail. Besides passing on information and squelching rumors, these calls and letters kept up morale.

Then, in September 1990, Dan Curtis landed Giant Eagle, the largest supermarket chain in the Pittsburgh area, which had taken note of the December snowstorm. Curtis took a group of its executives to the Gold Medal Bakery in New England, where a few years before he had developed a marketing system that would serve as a model. City Pride, he told them, would guarantee delivery of bread hot from its Pittsburgh ovens, with a better taste than the out-of-town bread that required emulsifiers as preservatives.

Tom Croft remembers an early meeting with one of Giant Eagle's top managers. "After we made our presentations, he said to us, 'You guys are pretty amazing. You don't have a bakery, you don't have a product, you don't have financing; you don't have anything. But I like what I see.' " The chain signed a letter of intent to buy City Pride bread packaged under the Giant Eagle name. That and commitments from other grocers convinced the City Pride people to forge ahead.

. . .

The search for adequate financing took another year. Meanwhile, a site was found on the banks of the Allegheny River in Lawrenceville, one of the oldest parts of Pittsburgh, and the shell of a building was started. For their part, the workers negotiated a wage contract that committed them to making less money than they had at Braun's, in exchange for partial ownership with the eventual option of buying out the other investors. By now, many were feeling the financial pinch. Wilma Harris got off work one day to find that her car had been repossessed. "But nobody gave up," says Harris. "Everybody who could came to the meetings, whether they were working or not."

The workers kept the heat on the city's politicians, too. In turn, Pittsburgh mayor Sophie Masloff made repeated phone calls to friends at Giant Eagle and the banks to keep them involved. Meanwhile, the character of City Pride was being formed. It was going to be a community-based company, extending a hand to the long-term unemployed, people on welfare, women and minorities, the handicapped, and simply those who wanted a job with a future. "We'll give anybody a chance," Chuck Geiger said. "We all know what it's like to be unemployed." The City Pride logo carried the words, "The bakery with a heart."

. . .

The summer of 1991 was an endless round of weekly meetings with the banks and representatives of public and private investors—a dizzying array of federal, state, county and city government agencies, unions, public utilities, community groups like the Lawrenceville Development Corporation, and more church groups like the Episcopal Investment Fund, as well as the chief investors, two venture capital investment firms. In all, some three dozen separate sources. But time was running out. "We had these deadlines," says Croft. "If we weren't able to close by the end of September, basically things were going to fall apart."

Most crucial was the deadline for the bakery machinery. After many disappointing searches, Ron Higgs, an equipment expert and now a City Pride investor, found just what they needed: a complete bread-and-roll equipment package about to go on auction in San Jose, California. City Pride could afford only used equipment, and even trying to put together separate machines from various sources was prohibitively expensive. This was the solution to their problem, but the equipment's owners wanted a payment. At the same time, the builders of the prospective bakery building were wondering if they shouldn't turn it into something else.

It all climaxed in an epic week at the end of September, as two dozen participants plus a lot of lawyers took over the first floor of one of the city's largest law firms for several days of frantic meetings. Croft, Curtis, Zajac, union leader Sam Papa, and Steven Zecher from the Urban Redevelopment Authority pulled one late-nighter after another, negotiating amid a flurry of faxes and phone calls and messengers ferrying documents in and out. In one case, a state senator drove the four hours from Harrisburg to hand-deliver a crucial document.

To keep nervous banks and investors from falling out, the City Pride advocates found themselves playing hardball. When they threatened a recalcitrant bank with a candlelight protest in the rain in front of its headquarters, the bank relented. Later, Dan Curtis pulled out the stops in a speaker-phone conference with an indecisive utility company. "Finally we were just screaming at the guy," Croft recalls. " 'If you don't do this, the whole project is going to collapse and we're going to let everybody know you caused it to collapse!' "

That company and the other backers stayed in. The marathon ended at about 7 P.M. on September 27, when the deal was sealed. The City Pride contingent promptly headed to the local bar to unwind.

Today, some of the City Pride workers do not discuss those three long years of unremitting struggle very easily. But when the topic turns to late 1991 and the days the 55 trucks rolled in with the bakery equipment, their eyes brighten and the words tumble out. With some up-front guidance from engineers, about 15 of them assembled the machinery that would be their bakery, filling a building longer than two football fields.

"I was the first one in here," says Joe Zajac. "I unloaded all the trucks and laid out the equipment. The building wasn't even finished yet."

"We worked 16-, 18-, 20-hour days, seven days a week, putting this machinery in," Richard Sipes says. "But it didn't bother us one bit. We really felt proud."

"People asked us why we were grinding the parts down, cleaning and repainting every piece," says Ali Deen. "Because it was ours." Says Sipes, "In six months' time we were taking tours around; they were asking me, 'This equipment is new, isn't it?' "

"That's how good it looked," Chuck Geiger says.

"That's how good it looked," Sipes agrees.

Then came the moment the former Braun's workers had been waiting for. For some, it was bittersweet—they had stayed with the group through three years of torturous uncertainty. Now, when the final commitment had to be made, some dropped out, mainly because they had other jobs they liked. But most didn't hesitate. Pearl Alexandre was back from Florida, ready to start. Wilma Harris quit her job at Nabisco, where she was making more than she would at City Pride and doing an easier job. "A lot of people tried to talk me out of it," she says. "But I'd seen it through this far; I wanted to see it succeed. And I knew it wouldn't work if we didn't have experienced people go in there to train the others."

In the end, 40 of the former Braun's workers walked into the new City Pride plant; they were joined by some 50 new hires, out of the 3,500 who applied, plus an administrative staff. "When we first came back here it was like being reunited with your family," Harris remembers. For two and a half months they worked the bugs out of the production process.

On September 10, 1992, City Pride had its grand opening. Along with the mayor and other officials, several workers were introduced, including Harris. "I didn't have to say anything—thank goodness," she laughs. The first person to speak was Pearl Alexandre. "Fifty-seven workers had a dream," she said. "Finally that small dream has now become real, a living part of our lives. . . . We conceived it. We believed it. We achieved it!"

They worked steadily from Saturday through early Monday morning, some of them 20 to 30 hours straight. City Pride baked its first bread for sale to the public on September 13, 1992, some 233,000 loaves that disappeared from supermarket shelves immediately.

Now they were back in their element: the flour-dusted factory floor, the big tubs of rising dough the buckets filled with shaped dough clattering along the labyrinthine line, the hot loaves and muffins emerging from the oven. Upstairs in his office, Dan Curtis breathed in the smell of the baking bread.

Their achievement was trumpeted in New York and Washington newspapers and on the major TV networks. And still, the story was not over.

As Tom Croft points out, eight out of ten start-up businesses fail in the first year, and City Pride came dangerously close to being one of the eight. By early 1993, the bakery's survival was once again in jeopardy. City and county officials got on the phone to the man who had rescued two other hometown companies when they seemed doomed—42-year-old Michael Carlow. Born in a nearby small town and now based in Pittsburgh, Carlow had bought the Pittsburgh Brewing Company (maker of a local icon, Iron City beer) and the D. L. Clark Candy Company (Pittsburgh-based maker of the national icon, the Clark Bar, since 1886) from outside owners and turned both into successful enterprises. These bold rescues had made Carlow something of a local hero. With deep pockets and a proven record of understanding Pittsburgh consumers, he was the natural choice.

In March 1993 a deal was struck. With new loans from the county and city, and backing from local banks, Carlow's Pittsburgh Food and Beverage bought City Pride. "I give the union and the workers credit for City Pride," Carlow says; "all the local people who wanted to make a statement, to keep a bakery in Pittsburgh and save jobs. What they underanticipated was the capital they needed to see it through."

"The most obvious disappointment was that the workers lost their ownership share, although they continue to participate in the bakery's management," says Croft. Many see a value to the trade-off. "This man taking over is the best thing for everybody," Richard Sipes says. "We feel more secure about our jobs."

Today, City Pride is supplying bread to two major local supermarket chains and buns for the hot dogs at Pittsburgh Pirates and Pittsburgh Steelers games at Three Rivers Stadium. It recently introduced its first product under the City Pride name: Roberto Bread, named for perhaps Pittsburgh's greatest sports hero, baseball great Roberto Clemente (*Smithsonian*, September 1993). More workers have been hired, and City Pride now looks forward to turning a profit in early 1994. "Just as they did with Pittsburgh Brewing and Clark Candy, the people of Pittsburgh have responded in a very positive way," says Michael Carlow.

Recently, some 500 unemployed bakery workers from Queens, New York, sent a contingent to visit City Pride. They are trying to start their own bakery, and are seeking the help of the workers and others who engineered the City Pride victory—the "largest community-development jobs project that I know of in the country, in terms of a grass-roots effort," says Tom Croft.

"When a plant closes," Croft continues, "the attitude usually is there's nothing we can do. But the City Pride workers said there is something you can do."

QUESTIONS FOR DISCUSSION AND ANALYSIS

Historically and Geographically/Globally Contextual

1. Briefly describe the history of Pittsburgh, as recounted in this story. What are the key structural processes in this story, and how are individuals affected by these processes?
2. How does this study compare to stories of other industrial plant closings in recent decades in the United States, such as automobile plant closings in Flint, Michigan; brewery closings in Milwaukee, Wisconsin; or textile and computer plant closings in California?
3. Why do corporations decide to close certain plants and open others? Why does this benefit them? Do workers have a say in these decisions? In what ways do these decisions affect workers?
4. Was it beneficial for these workers that the Braun's plant survived so long after the Pittsburgh steel mills had closed? If the Braun's plant had closed a decade or two earlier, would the Pittsburgh community have supported the creation of City Pride?
5. Historically, unions have been important advocates for workers' rights. What importance did union membership have for Braun's workers?

Socially Constructed

6. Factory workers who lose their jobs are often depicted as powerless "others" and/or as victims of social structures. Workers are typically not seen as having the agency to determine their own lives. How are the City Pride workers constructed in Kowinski's story?
7. What did the City Pride workers think of themselves? What do you think Croft or Curtis or Carlow thought of them? What did the Pittsburgh community think of them? Why are these impressions important?

8. Wilma Harris, Pearl Alexandre, and Ali Deen were all African American. However, Joe Zajac, Tom Croft, Dan Curtis, and Michael Carlow at least appear to be White (with various ethnic backgrounds) from photos of the City Pride efforts. The former group are workers and all of the latter group have management responsibilities. What are the implications of this story for racial and class hierarchies? Are these hierarchies challenged, reinforced, or both?

9. This story is written to highlight the successes of City Pride. What indications do we have that the story might not have always been so positive? What downfalls did the Braun's workers have, and what roadblocks did the creators of City Pride run into? What barriers do they still confront and why?

10. How might we view City Pride if the race, class, or gender of the people involved were different? For instance, would we have heard a different story if Dan Curtis or Michael Carlow had been African American or Asian American? Would Wilma Harris have had more say in the coalition if she had been White?

11. How might the workers be viewed if we knew some of them were gays or lesbians? Why is sexuality ignored in this story? We can gather information on the race, class, and gender of each of the workers, managers, and chairpersons, but why do we know nothing of their sexuality?

Power Relationships

12. Who has the socially sanctioned race, class, gender, and sexuality power in the creation of City Pride?

13. In what ways did the Braun's workers challenge oppression?

14. Did the City Pride workers reach their goals? If so, what goals did they achieve? Were existing power relations challenged?

15. What goals of the City Pride workers were not achieved? Why?

16. Why didn't Wilma, Ali, Pearl, or Joe try to secure better jobs after the Braun's plant closed? Why were they so determined to get their same jobs back?

17. Did any of the workers' actions reinforce power relations in society? Did any of Curtis's, Carlow's, or Croft's actions reinforce existing power relations? If so, how?

18. Which groups gain the most from the success of City Pride—former Braun's workers, former Braun's managers, Pittsburgh grocery store chains, or consultants like Tom Croft? Which groups lose?

Macro/Social Structural and Micro/Social Psychological Levels

19. How does this story highlight both macro-structural processes and micro-level, everyday processes in people's lives?

20. What types of institutional/macro structures might have led Ralston Purina to fire 110 workers and to close the Braun's plant?

21. How did the workers turn an unfortunate incident on the macro level into a beneficial micro-level experience? Discuss the connections between the plant's closing and the workers' ability to collectively resist and to boost morale and self-worth within their own lives.

22. In what ways have Michael Carlow or Dan Curtis always had different opportunities and experiences from those of Wilma Harris or Ali Deen? In what ways will they continue to have different opportunities and experiences? Compared to the workers, for instance, how are Carlow or Curtis affected by the success of City Pride?

23. Do the City Pride workers face any type of institutional discrimination? Were they faced with stereotypes that hindered or restricted their success in the creation of a new bakery?

Simultaneously Expressed

24. How does the simultaneous oppression of race, class, and gender affect Ali's, Pearl's, and Wilma's lives differently from others' in the story?

25. Would Wilma's position be different if she were a lesbian? Would Dan's position have been different if he had been gay?

26. Can we say that class is the primary oppression in these workers' lives? Can we say that class is the primary privilege in Dan Curtis's or Michael Carlow's lives? Why or why not?

27. How does the assumption of heterosexuality in this story work to benefit all individuals portrayed?

28. What collective and individual dreams are evident in this story? In what ways are these dreams consistent with what we might expect, given the social locations of individuals in this story?

Implications for Social Action and Social Justice

29. Why is it important that 57 workers acted as a group to resist the Braun's plant's closing? Why is collective resistance more successful in many cases than individual acts of resistance?

30. How was the refusal to leave Pittsburgh a challenge to existing power structures? How was it also a result of various dimensions of oppression in workers' lives?

31. How is the City Pride story different from, yet similar, to other factory closings in the United States? How can this comparison inform U. S. economic or labor policy?

32. What were the keys to City Pride's success? Or was it pure luck that City Pride got off the ground? Could this story be reproduced in another city at another time?

REFERENCES

Bamberger, Bill and Cathy N. Davidson. 1998. *Closing: The Life and Death of an American Factory.* Durham, NC: Center for Documentary Studies; New York: W.W. Norton.

Dandaneau, Steven P. 1996. *A Town Abandoned: Flint, Michigan Confronts Deindustrialization.* Albany, NY: State University of New York.

Fantasia, Rick. 1988. *Cultures of Solidarity: Consciousness, Action and Contemporary American Workers.* Berkeley, CA: University of California Press.

Hamper, Bill. 1991. *Rivethead: Tales from the Assembly Line.* New York: Warner.

Illes, Louise M. 1996. *Sizing Down: Chronicle of a Plant Closing.* Ithaca: ILR Press.

Jones, Jacqueline. 1998. *American Work: Four Centuries of Black and White Labor.* New York: W.W. Norton.

Kelley, Robin. 1994. *Race Rebels: Culture, Politics, and the Black Working Class.* New York: Free Press.

Kowinski, William Severini. 1993. "The Tale of City Pride." *Smithsonian* 24(7), pp. 118–132.

Krepps, Matthew B. and Amy Bertin Candell. 1997. *Industrial Inefficiency and Downsizing: A Study of Layoffs and Plant Closures.* New York: Garland Publishers.

Naples, Nancy A. (Ed.). 1998. *Community Activism and Feminist Politics: Organizing across Race, Class, and Gender.* New York: Routledge.

Soltero, José M. 1996. *Inequality in the Workplace: Underemployment among Mexicans, African Americans, and Whites.* New York: Garland Publishing, Inc.

Punishing Institutions: The Story of Catherine (Cedar Woman)[1]

Luana Ross

Our family was large, but it was seldom that you ever got a hug. If you did, you were grateful for it.
                                                                        —Catherine

Introduction

I met Catherine in 1990, at the Women's Correctional Center in Montana. She is currently serving a forty year sentence and is housed at the women's prison in Billings. When Catherine was first arrested, the local media used a simplistic Adam and Eve theory and presented her as a controlling woman and the driving force behind the crime. In reality, Catherine's "crime" was that she was present when the horrendous murder of a young white man was committed. A plea bargain was arranged and she was charged with a lesser crime, not kidnapping and homicide, with the stipulation that she provide testimony against her male co-defendants, who are members of her tribe.

At her sentencing, the judge asked her if she realized why she was sentenced to prison. A bewildered Catherine replied, "No." According to Catherine, the judge responded: "Because you were aware of a crime in progress and did nothing to stop it; therefore, you are just as guilty because you allowed this to happen." Although Catherine did not commit the murder, she lives everyday with the guilt of not halting the crime, as though she could have possibly had the authority to stop two powerfully violent men from killing a young man. To date, Catherine has been in prison for nine years and has been continually denied parole. Because of the seriousness of the crime, in conjunction with the dynamics of racism in the state of Montana, Catherine believes that she is singled out by prison staff and the parole board, and subsequently issued racialized harassment.

Catherine wants her story to be heard because she is committed to breaking the silence of violence and exposing its psychological toll, especially on children. Nevertheless, her identity is disguised in an effort to protect members of her family. Catherine's narrative, only a glimpse into a life filled with turbulence, is based on interviews conducted from 1991 to 1994 and data from legal papers, prison records, newspapers, and personal correspondence.

. . .

[1]Luana Ross, "Punishing Institutions: The Story of Catherine (Cedar Woman)" (edited). Copyright © 1996 by Luana Ross. Reprinted with the permission of the author.

Catherine, Cedar Woman (her Indian name), was born in a log house and grew up on one of Montana's seven Indian reservations. She was raised in a traditional Native American family by members of her extended family. Catherine fluently speaks both her Native language and English, although she is more comfortable conversing in her Native tongue. Of her early life and the wisdom of elders, Catherine comments:

> I grew up on the reservation and lived with extended family members, and attended a Catholic boarding school. My grandmother often shared with me that our Mother Earth is the caretaker for [God]. Also, when other Indian elders talked about visions, I had doubts and wondered if their visions and predictions were true just like any other child would question and wonder. My grandmother, and other elders of neighboring reservations, made predictions during my youth that are now coming true. They raised me to believe in the Native American Church and I learned to maintain my focus on [God] through any situation. We have learned to have faith in [God] through living life and learning to survive. This journey in life helps us to learn; and at some point we have a spiritual awakening that helps us identify that, the freedom we are all seeking is within.

Catherine has four sisters and four brothers; one sister and two brothers are deceased. Another brother was adopted by a white family, and the two have never met. She attended a Catholic Indian boarding school, married at a young age, and began having children.

On the surface, it appears that Catherine was raised in a traditional and functional family; however, this is not the case. Catherine never mentions her father and has many negative memories of her mother. Often Catherine's mother was drinking when she would visit her, which greatly displeased other family members. As a child, Catherine rarely saw her mother. What she remembers most about her mother, aside from her drinking, was that she did not appear to like Catherine. She said: "It seemed like she didn't like me. There was no physical contact—like you give your kids a hug and stuff. She never did do that. She would just sit and look at me. She just kind of floated in and out. And the times that she did show up, she was always with white guys. I didn't even know she was my mom. I thought my aunt was my mom."

As Catherine matured she witnessed her uncle physically abuse other family members, including her aunt and her grandmother. She became increasingly angry with her biological mother and, furthermore, reasoned that brutality was an acceptable behavior:

> I was angry at my real mom because she was my mom and she drank all the time. I just didn't want anything from her. And then I just kind of continued in my little life with that and feeling angry. When I would see my mother, I would let this anger show. Then I started treating her like how I seen my uncle treating my aunt. You know, when my aunt and uncle would go drinking, well when they came back home my uncle would beat her up all the time. There were so many times. I don't know if my brother remembers it, but I always do. We would be the only ones awake and we would watch my uncle.

He beat her so many times that sometimes you wouldn't recognize her the next day. And they walked around like nothing happened. . . . I felt funny. I don't know how the other kids felt but I remember feeling real funny. And, I just put my head down and started eating. Then I looked at my grandma and I looked at my aunt. Then my uncle came in and he sat down and started talking. They were all visiting with one another like nothing was going on. You know, like nothing had happened! So then I started thinking that nothing was wrong.

The upheaval and family secrets continued as Catherine grew. She witnessed not only the brutality between her aunt and uncle, she also saw her uncle and biological mother beat her grandmother. Remembering a family thoroughly and painfully immersed in violence, she said: "And he [her uncle] said, 'I'm going to kill your daughter.' And he was just hollering at my grandmother. And they talk about respect for the elders now. And then they wonder why this generation and the ones to come don't have respect for the elders. You learn what you see. I watched my real mother break my grandmother's arm." Despite the turmoil, Catherine's grandmother encouraged her to pray for strength and to leave the reservation. According to Catherine, her grandmother said: "Go somewhere else and learn what's going on out there. Don't be like the rest of them and don't stay around here—it's no good now." To this elder Native woman, the good old days were gone and the reservation grew increasingly violent.

Catherine was eight years old when her uncle began sexually abusing her. Her aunt, rather than stopping the transgression, allowed it to continue. Catherine remembers: "My aunt came and laid down with me one night and she was stroking my hair. I was just a little girl—about eight. She was laying there with me and she was stroking my hair. Then my uncle climbed in bed on the other side and I remember her saying, 'Just lay still and it won't hurt—it'll be OK.' These are the people that loved me; these are the one's I trusted [crying]." Because Catherine's aunt did little to stop the rapes—when her aunt intervened she was abused by her tyrannical husband—she soon became angry with her. As an adult, Catherine discovered that her aunt was taking "sleeping pills" to cope with her own oppression and, subsequently, had little initiative and clearly no power to stop her husband from terrorizing the household.

According to Catherine, her extended family took care of her and her brother, not because of love, but out of a twisted sense of responsibility and family obligation. Catherine watched her family's collapse, which left her feeling insignificant and frustrated:

> You know how you watch the wind blowing? It slowly keeps blowing something apart? Maybe you watch it loosening the dirt and it just keeps blowing away a little bit at a time. That's how I seen our family. My grandmother started drinking. I was just slowly watching everything go and when you're a small child growing up watching all of this, it's scary. I can't think of no other word to make it sound easier, softer. It's just plain scary. And nobody to ever talk to. You see, these adults are people that you come to depend on. They're suppose to know what they're doing; they're the smart ones, you know.

During Catherine's childhood, she was shuffled between various relatives and Indian boarding school. One proposed alternative was to live with her mother, who was drinking heavily and frequently physically abused Catherine and her brother. Catherine's stays with her mother were always short-lived. She preferred to live with her grandmother, but ill health and old age prevented a long-term placement. The family secrets and the silence were unbearable to Catherine, and at age twelve she began skipping school and drinking as a way to numb her pain: "I just felt like I was better off being in my own little drunk world and then I didn't have to think about these things anymore. I knew sooner or later that I would pass out and then I'd forget about it—until I sobered up again."

Witnessing men abuse women provoked a pattern in Catherine's life. Not unexpectedly, Catherine was involved in remarkably abusive relationships with men:

> That's the only thing I knew. Someone would beat me up and I thought they loved me. And this man did both; he beat me up and he used me in a bad way—in a sexual way. And he was telling me he loved me, and I'd listen to him. The way I was raised, I watched my aunt and no matter how bad they got beat up, they still listened to their husbands. You know, this is what I learned. Then all of a sudden my aunt's saying, "Why do you do that? Why do you let these men beat you up and you always go right back to him?' That's what I'm talking about. They're giving that advice away but they're doing it themselves.

One of the men Catherine was involved with was the man who committed the murder that landed her in prison. Not surprisingly, their relationship was extremely abusive and she lived in continual fear of this man: "I started living with him just about a couple of months before we got in trouble [arrested for the murder]. My kids were scared of him and I was really scared of this man. He beat my ex-husband up really bad. . . . He was going to shoot my ex-husband . . . and I begged and pleaded with him and I promised him, 'I'll do anything you ask—just don't do that.' " Describing a remarkably controlling person, she continues: "I couldn't go anywhere by myself—he'd always come with me, even when I went to the bathroom."

Catherine's co-defendants, as well as some tribal members, viewed her testimony against them as "snitching." To Catherine, however, she was merely telling the truth. Remembering prior beatings and intimidation, she was intensely afraid of her boyfriend (her co-defendant) and consequently unable to make a decision regarding her testimony. Family members prayed with her in jail and instructed her on honesty, a virtue in her tribe. According to Catherine, they told her: "We always taught you never to lie; we taught you to be honest. This is how you were raised. You were raised in the Indian way and that's one of the things is when you are Indian, you should not lie. We told you that. If you know something, you'd better say something."

Catherine was still confused about the role of her testimony and the label "snitch." That night she had a dream that aided in her decision to tell the truth:

> I went to bed and I was sleeping. All of a sudden, I felt really cold. And I was in that cell—that little tiny cell. All of a sudden, I just felt like someone was with me. Pretty soon, it got warm. And then I was sitting on a small couch and my grandmother was sitting there. My mother was there and she was holding my hand, but she wasn't saying anything. When I looked over, my other grandmother was sitting kitty-corner from us. Then my two grandfathers were there. One of my grandfathers lost part of his toes due to frost-bite, so he used a cane. When I looked at him, he was doing like I always saw him at home. He was bouncing his cane off the floor and he was singing real low. My other grandfather was sitting behind him. He seemed like he was listening to my other grandfather. Out of my whole family, my grandmother was the one that always did the talking. I mean, when you heard her voice you knew to be quiet. She was talking and leaning over this way. She said, 'When we raised you, we told you when times get really hard to pray. This is how we raised you. We told you that but somewhere along the way, I think you forgot. I always talk to you.' Then she turned around and said, 'Here, you take this—you're going to need this.' And she gave me a piece of cloth. Then she said, 'Where you're going, you're going to need this. This is going to help you.' Then she turned back around and she said, 'We raised you kids right and we always told you to tell the truth. You were raised the hard way, but that was for a reason.' She was talking in [Native language]. She said, 'We always tell you, don't be crying.' I was listening and she turned around and gave me a sandwich. She said, 'We told you to pray. Sometimes you have a hard walk. When you get hungry, this is for you.' And I turned around and saw my sister [who is deceased]. She was laughing and she said, 'Remember we'll always love you.' I turned around and put the stuff on a little table behind me. When I turned back around, I was all alone. There was no one there and all of a sudden that warm feeling just started going away and I got really cold again. Then I woke up. I sat there and thought and thought. So that's what helped me make my decision.

Divinely inspired, Catherine made the decision to tell the truth about the crime. That her instructions to do so came in the form of a dream/vision, renders the notion of "snitching" sacrilegious.

More Prisons, More Violence

Because Catherine has been incarcerated for such a lengthy time, she has a keen idea regarding control and punishment. As well, she is cognizant of the racism working within institutional structures. For instance, Catherine was sent to a Catholic Indian boarding school and experienced what she terms a transformation from Indian to Catholic:

> I became aware of disparate treatment years ago when I experienced incarceration after being convicted of an alcohol-related crime, and my experiences in Catholic boarding school. Although some acts of discrimination did not point to race, it suggested indifference toward Indians due to beliefs, traditions, and religions. Addressing issues of discrimination partially refers to Catholic priests and nuns who dictated the attempted conversion of Indians to Christians.

Intensely spiritual, Catherine relies on her Native religion to aid in her survival of the violence in her life prior to her incarceration and the violence of prisonization. She recalls the words of the aunt who raised her: "No matter what they have done, there is always a reason why people do the things they do but there is a solution at the end of every situation and we will all grow from it. And remember to pray before you begin any project because what you put into that project is what you will give to the people."

Similar to many other Native people, Catherine suggests that Native American culture, specifically prayer, gives Native people the strength to endure seemingly insurmountable events. In an effort to analyze discrimination, she questions specifically why Native Americans were subjected to genocidal practices. In an essay she wrote:

> Are Indians targeted in boarding schools and prisons simply because they have their own culture and religion? Does the fact that Indians have strong beliefs, traditions and upbringing make them a challenge for those obsessed to convert them? Perhaps trying to gain control by diverting the Indians attention to a man on the cross and attempting to convince them that their belief in the eagle and Great Grandfather is false or voodoo. Skillfully and manipulatively, authority figures use Indian beliefs in reverse psychology. In this way they gain a false trust, therefore, enabling a slow elimination of Native traditions forcing them to convert to their rules and non-Indian ways.

Catherine recognizes that early efforts to "civilize" and "educate" Native Americans were controlling and punishing. She said: "My memories of Catholic boarding school is one of strict discipline. Military style methods doled out to little Indian children once we were out-of-sight of our parents and grandparents. Little Indian children who could no longer speak Indian nor practice Indian ways were being punished for living their heritage and not allowed to discuss any of the school's disciplinary practices when they went home for visits." Catherine describes the strict regime they encountered as children:

> Disciplinary methods imposed on Indian children by nuns and priests consisted of sitting in the walk-in freezer an hour or more, hitting a brick wall twenty to thirty times with your fists (depending upon the infraction), or kneeling for hours and praying after they made us attend confession. Once four of us little girls would not say the Hail Mary and the Sister Superior marched us into a room and spanked us with a thick wide leather strap until our behinds bled. Then we had to memorize the Hail Mary as part of the sanction, which included attending confession for our disobedience to God. Another occurrence was when some Indian boys stepped out of line and were taken outside to hit the brick building with their fists. They were brought back into class after hitting the brick wall. They were crying and the tops of their hands were cut open and bleeding profusely. They wore bandages on their hands for awhile.

Of course, many Native people resisted such deplorable treatment. It is well known that many escaped by running away from boarding school. Catherine relates just such an experience and the harsh penalties doled out by supposed servants of the Lord:

> A haunting memory of my cousin and her friend who escaped the boarding school left scars that have helped to develop certain fears which strongly influenced future behaviors. The school, with assistance from the police, organized a manhunt and upon finding them returned them to school for disciplinary action with no notification to the parents. Their sanction, without a hearing, consisted of time-out in a walk-in freezer in the cafeteria and for everyone to view them while we eat our meal. Their sanction lasted approximately two and a half hours. After they were released from the freezer, my friend and I helped them to warm up. My cousin shared with me, while I was rubbing her hands and legs, that they attempted to bring back chokecherries for us. But the cherries were taken away and they were told that this was a bad thing and they would have to be punished because they needed to eat healthier foods. The time-out in the freezer depended upon the infraction, and I witnessed some children held in the freezer longer than two hours.

One of the connections Catherine has made is the incredible similarities in Indian boarding schools and the penal system. An introspective journey enabled Catherine to link her past experiences of abuse to her present experiences in the criminal justice system. As a woman who has been incarcerated for many years, Catherine conclusively understands the prison system as biased against Native people. Additionally, she is well aware of the punishing efforts that exist in a system specifically designed as punitive, although operating under the guise of "rehabilitation."

Regarding the prison's dehumanizing classification process, Catherine said: "The prison system will process individuals by taking all their clothing, jewelry, and any personal items and by conducting a thorough strip search checking all cavity areas for any contraband. Usually the cavity searches are at the discretion of the officers. After the search, they delouse the person with lice shampoo and you are showered and issued your prison attire of a white gown with slippers for your feet. They lock the individual into an intake room for two weeks to a month, depending upon the classification and the conviction. After the classification process, a number is issued and the person is taken to their proper classification unit or allowed in the prison population."

According to Catherine, Indian boarding school had a similar degrading entrance process:

> I recall how we had to line up to be deloused. The awful smells of lice shampoo and the haircuts. Little white T-shirts and cotton panties and later cotton pajamas. Everything was white or dark blue and we marched around like little soldiers. For awhile, we wore dark blue uniforms—blue skirts with vests and white shirts. I do not recall what took place when they allowed us to wear our own clothing, although this came probably after I entered the fourth grade. Standing at attention like little soldiers—very still—not daring to flinch or even blink.

The dehumanizing ritual—whether it was Indian boarding school or prison—started with stripping, delousing, and the wearing of uniforms. The regime in prison, similar to boarding school, is militaristically fashioned. Catherine said that today in the women's prison one stands for the prison count "at 6 A.M., 11 A.M., and 3:30 P.M. and if anyone misses count or is considered dis-ruptive, a disciplinary is issued. I remember in the boarding school days how we had to stand at the foot of our beds for morning and night count."

The oppression of the prison system, particularly for Native women, has been noted (Ross 1993, 1994, 1996, 1997; Sugar and Fox 1990). Prisoners are often left to the discretion of the guards and jailers. Catherine reminisces about being in jail with a relative and the frightful exercise of authority:

> I sat in my cell one night visiting with an uncle who was in the next cell and talking between the wall when we heard keys jingling and doors open. I heard the officers' voices on the other side of the cell block talking to someone—asking questions. The individual said he had nothing to say. Suddenly an offi-cer began raising his voice saying he was going to teach him to do as they told him and never to disagree. Then I heard the sounds of loud slaps—the sounds of someone hitting a person. I heard sounds like someone hitting the wall and then crying. The man asked them to stop—that he had had enough. The slaps didn't stop until only a moan and then dead silence. The only sound was the hum of the air and space in the cell block. The beating lasted for approxi-mately twenty minutes. Sitting quietly, my uncle whispers to me the words of advice from someone more experienced about incarceration. "You act like you never heard nothing and you say nothing. When they [the jailers] come and ask you anything, you smile and tell them it's good to see them and you are doing good."

They relocated Catherine's uncle to another jail. Now she was alone and exceedingly vulnerable as she awaited her trial. Sleepless over the loss of free-dom and her family, in addition to the maliciousness of the crime, it was dur-ing this time that she was raped by a jailer. And not raped just once, but seven times over a period of three and a half months. In an effort to spare herself emotionally, Catherine methodically reports one rape:

> He [the jailer] took me into the office and told me to be quiet. He told me to lay down on the floor. He said he had something he wanted to try. He had a red condom. He put this on himself and pulled my shorts off. He raped me. When he finished, he stood there laughing at me. Then he went and got a towel and cleaned himself off. He told me to get dressed and then he sat down and told me to do oral sex on him. He told me to get on my knees and then he grabbed me by the face and started pushing his penis into my mouth until he ejaculated. Then he let go of me. He again laughed at me. He took me back to my cell, locked it, and left.

In an intimidating manner, the jailer told Catherine she better not say any-thing because he had much to lose and no one would believe her anyway. She was, after all, a Native woman and he was a white male with much power and authority. As the rapes continued, Catherine thought she might be pregnant but was afraid to tell anyone. Fortunately, she was not carrying a child. Al-though Catherine eventually raised the issue of her rape by the jailer to vari-ous authorities, nothing was done. In fact, similar to countless other women who are raped while incarcerated, no one believed her.

Because of the brutality in Catherine's life, she is repulsed by violence. She continues to have nightmares about the rapes, beatings, and crime of which she was eventually convicted. She is unable to watch violent movies on television or read about violence because it nauseates her. The sexual intimidation that presently exists in prison (see Ross 1994, 1997), particularly because of her history, repels her. Recognizing the hypocrisy of the criminal justice system, Catherine said: "The part that really bothers me is when I look around the prison. All these workers, you know, we're under their care. We're under their custody. They're the ones that have the lock and key. . . . And they have the nerve to talk about law and order; and they have the audacity to talk about discipline."

Women are particularly vulnerable in the criminal justice system and another issue that is gender specific is the hysterectomies that occurred while Catherine was incarcerated at the Women's Correctional Center (see Ross 1997). Of this form of violence, Catherine said:

> Recalling a personal situation, and as witness to other women experiencing the same, between 1988–1992 there were a great number of hysterectomies within the women's prison. They were referring women for hysterectomies regularly. Without any information presented and the only solutions for the medical problems pertaining to women's monthly cycle or cervical complications, which could have had a simple remedy other than major surgery. The process of my own surgery developed into a debate with the nurse, which eventually resulted into threats of a disciplinary and strong rebuttal to my Indian upbringing. No other remedy or alternative was ever presented except the surgery. It was discovered later that the uterus was in healthy condition with no scarring or spots when inspected, according to my medical reports.

Before the surgery, Catherine argued with a prison nurse and guard, who escorted her to a room and tried to convince her of the "needed" operation. Additionally, they instructed her to "let go" of her Native beliefs because they would not help her. Catherine reasoned that she needed to see an Indian doctor for severe menstrual cramps and heavy bleeding. According to Catherine, the nurse screamed at her and said: "To hell with your traditions and beliefs. This is a medical issue."

The issue of denial of culture is noteworthy. Although the American Indian Religious Freedom Act was passed in 1978 to ensure that Native cultures could be freely practiced (including while one is incarcerated), there is little or no compliance at the Women's Correctional Center (Ross 1994, 1996, 1997). Catherine sent a memo to the chemical dependency counselor regarding her denial of religion. Because sweetgrass and sage were believed by some prison staff to be drugs, she asked the counselor to please offer a cultural-awareness workshop for the staff. White prisoners, as well as prison staff (who are all white), are ignorant of Native culture and frequently refer to Native religion as "voo-doo" (for a thorough analysis see Ross 1996, 1997). In the memo to prison staff it was reported by Catherine that, "One inmate stated to me she has been told by another inmate that Native Americans are fooling staff by

telling them we call this sweetgrass when what we have is really opium."
Catherine finds much solace in her Native culture, although the full practice is
denied by prison staff. Evidently, within the prison Native culture is viewed
as a liability, not a strength.

. . .

QUESTIONS FOR DISCUSSION AND ANALYSIS

Historically and Geographically/Globally Contextual

1. Native Americans lived in the United States before any other group, yet
   they are one of the least powerful groups in America. What historical
   processes and policies have characterized the colonial experience of Native Americans? How are they evident in Catherine's life?
2. When and why did the "boarding school" practice of removing Native
   American children from their homes and cultures for schooling originate?
   What is the historical impact of this practice on native people and how has
   it affected Catherine's life?
3. From Catherine's story does it appear that Native Americans have gained
   greater rights over the past few decades?
4. How did growing up on a reservation affect Catherine's life? How would
   her life have been different had she grown up outside a reservation? How
   might her brothers' lives be different from her life?

Socially Constructed

5. How is Native American culture characterized by the media and dominant American culture? For instance, how do Catherine's jailers or other
   inmates view Native American women? Do these characterizations influence their behavior towards Catherine?
6. How did Indian boarding schools attempt to deconstruct Native American
   identity in children? What new identity were Catherine and other children
   expected to adopt?
7. How has Catherine's experience of abuse influenced her definitions of
   family and love?
8. How is the social construction of gender in Native American culture similar to or different from that of the dominant culture?
9. How is age socially constructed in the Native American community? Is
   this construction different from or similar to the ways in which age is socially constructed in other U.S. communities?

Power Relationships

10. How do power relationships of race, class, gender, and sexuality manifest
    in Catherine's history of physical and sexual abuse?

11. How did Catherine resist dominant groups' power at various points in her life? Do any of Catherine's actions reinforce power structures of race, class, gender, or sexuality? If so, how?
12. In some cases, Catherine has been encouraged by family members to appear passive and powerless. Why? Does this benefit her? Can silence or stoicism sometimes be a strategy for gaining social power?
13. Why didn't Catherine speak out about sexual and physical abuse earlier or more often? Why is she speaking out now?
14. What questions does this story raise about the power relations between researcher and subject? About their responsibilities to one another? What conflicts may Catherine and Luana Ross have had to face in deciding to tell Catherine's story? What did each stand to gain or lose?
15. Is Catherine aware of the power relationships of race, class, gender, and sexuality operating within her life? How do you know?

Macro/Social Structural and Micro/Social Psychological Levels

16. How are race, class, gender, and sexuality hierarchies in education, criminal justice, and religion evident in Catherine's life?
17. Catherine compares her experience in prison to her experience in boarding schools. How have these institutions worked together to shape Catherine's life?
18. Why did Catherine stay with abusive husbands/boyfriends?
19. Consider the importance of religious institutions in Catherine's life—both positive and negative influences.
20. Studies on gendered sentencing practices document differential treatment of women and men in the criminal court system. Think about Catherine's sentence of 40 years for witnessing (and not stopping) a murder. What are the institutional processes of race, class, gender, and sexuality that might explain why she may be serving such a long sentence? If Catherine had been middle class and White or the victim had been Native American, do you think she would have been serving 40 years? Why?
21. The White guard warns Catherine not to tell about the rapes, saying that he "has a lot to lose." What could a White man have to lose if someone believed Catherine? What macro-level forces could be influencing his life? And if he did have "a lot to lose," why did he risk raping Catherine? What macro- and micro-level factors might explain this rape?

Simultaneously Expressed

22. How have systems of race, class, gender, and sexuality simultaneously affected Catherine and her family's life?
23. If we assume that abuse is the result of only gender discrimination, what situations or contexts might we miss in analyzing Catherine's experiences?
24. In what ways are Catherine's social location and criminal status linked?

25. What dimensions of oppression or privilege currently seem most promi-
    nent in Catherine's life? Have they changed over time? What structures of
    oppression seem least apparent in her life? Why?
26. Physical and sexual violence is interconnected with systems of oppression.
    Discuss both why the men in Catherine's life abused and why the women
    and children were abused.

Implications for Social Action and Social Justice

27. Catherine wanted her story to be heard. What does story-telling have to
    do with activism?
28. Who might Catherine's audience be? If she reaches them, what difference
    will it make?
29. How might Catherine's story be used in efforts to combat violence against
    women?
30. How could Luana Ross's interview with Catherine be a model for other
    interviewing projects? What ethical questions does it present?

REFERENCES

Awiakta, Marilou. 1993. *Selu: Seeking the Corn Mother's Wisdom.* Golden, CO:
    Fulcrum Publishing.
Jacobs, Sue-Ellen, Wesley Thomas, and Sabine Lang (Eds.). 1997. *Two-Spirit
    People: Native American Gender Identity, Sexuality, and Spirituality.* Urbana,
    IL: University of Illinois Press.
Lobo, Susan and Steve Talbot (Eds.). 1998. *Native American Voices: A Reader.*
    New York: Longman.
Miller, Susan L. (Ed.). 1998. *Crime Control and Women: Feminist Implications of
    Criminal Justice Policy.* Thousand Oaks, CA: Sage Publications, Inc.
Ross, Luana. 1998. *Inventing the Savage: The Social Construction of Native
    American Criminality.* Austin, TX: University of Texas Press.

CASE STUDY 5

The Girl Who Wouldn't Sing[1]

Kit Yuen Quan

. . . People assume that I don't have a language problem because I can speak English, even when I ask them to take into account that English is my second language. This is the usual reaction I have gotten while working in the feminist movement. It's true that my language problems are different from those of a recent immigrant who cannot work outside of Chinatown because she or he doesn't speak enough English. Unlike my parents, I don't speak with a heavy accent. After twenty years of living in this country, watching American television and going through its school system, I have acquired adequate English skills to function fairly well. I can pass as long as I don't have to write anything or say what I really think around those whom I see as being more educated and articulate than I am. I can spend the rest of my life avoiding jobs that require extensive reading and writing skills. I can join the segment of the population that reads only out of necessity rather than for information, appreciation or enlightenment.

It's difficult for people to accept that I believe I have a literacy problem because they do not understand the nature of my blocks with language. Learning anything new terrifies me, especially if it involves words or writing. I get this overwhelming fear, this heart-stopping panic that I won't understand it. I won't know how to do it. My body tenses up and I forget to breathe if there is a word in a sentence that I don't know or several sentences in a paragraph containing unfamiliar words. My confidence dwindles and I start to feel the ground falling from under me. In my frustration I feel like crying, running out or smashing something, but that would give me away, expose my defect. So I tune out or nod my head as if there is nothing wrong. I've had to cover it up in order to survive, get jobs, pass classes and at times to work and live with people who do not care to understand my reality.

Living with this fear leaves me exhausted. I feel backed against a wall of self-doubt, pushed into a corner, defeated, unable to stretch or take advantage of opportunities. Beyond just being able to read and write well enough to get by, I need to be able to learn, understand, communicate, to articulate my thoughts and feelings, and participate fully without feeling ashamed of who I am and where I come from.

When I first arrived in San Francisco from Hong Kong at age seven and a half, the only English I knew was the alphabet and a few simple words: cat,

[1]Kit Yuen Quan, "The Girl Who Wouldn't Sing" (excerpted) from Gloria Anzaldua, ed., *Making Face, Making Soul, Haciendo Caras: Creative and Critical Perspectives by Feminists of Color.* Copyright © 1990 by Kit Yuen Quan. Copyright © 1990 by Gloria Anzaldua. Reprinted with the permission of Aunt Lute Books.

53

dog, table, chair. I sat in classrooms for two to three years without under-standing what was being said, and cried while the girl next to me filled in my spelling book for me. In music class when other kids volunteered to go up in front of the class to play musical instruments, I'd never raise my hand. I wouldn't sing. The teacher probably wondered why there were always three Chinese girls in one row who wouldn't sing. In art class, I was so traumatized that I couldn't be creative. While other kids moved about freely in school, seeming to flow from one activity to the next, I was disoriented, out of step, feeling hopelessly behind. I went into a "survivor mode" and couldn't partici-pate in activities.

I remember one incident in particular in the fourth grade during a kickball game. I had just missed the ball when Kevin, the class jock, came running across the yard and kicked me in the butt. Had I been able to speak English, I might have screamed my head off or called for the teacher, but I just stood there trying to numb out the pain, feeling everyone's eyes on me. I wasn't sure it wasn't all part of the game.

At home I spoke the sam yup dialect of Cantonese with my parents, who were completely unaware of the severity of my problems at school. In their eyes I was very lucky to be going to school in America. My father had had only a high school education before he had to start working. And we children would not have had any chance to go to college had we stayed in Hong Kong. We had flown over the Pacific Ocean three times between the time I was seven and a half and eight and a half because they were so torn about leaving their home to resettle in a foreign country and culture. At the dinner table after a day of toiling at their jobs and struggling with English, they aired their frus-trations about the racism and discrimination they were feeling everywhere: at their jobs, on the bus, at the supermarket. Although they didn't feel very hope-ful about their own lives, they were comforted by the fact that my brother and I were getting a good education. Both my parents had made incredible sacri-fices for my education. Life would be easier for us, with more opportunities and options, because we would know the language. We would be able to talk back or fight back if need be. All we had to do was study hard and apply our-selves. So every day after school I would load my bag full of textbooks and walk up two hills to where we lived the first few years after we landed here. I remember opening each book and reading out loud a paragraph or two, skip-ping over words I didn't know until I gave up in frustration.

My parents thought that by mastering the English language, I would be able to attain the Chinese American dream: a college education, a good-paying job, a house in the suburbs, a Chinese husband and children. They felt intimi-dated and powerless in American society and so clung tightly to me to fulfill their hopes and dreams. When I objected to these expectations using my lim-ited Chinese, I received endless lectures. I felt smothered by their traditional values of how a Chinese girl should behave and this was reason enough not to learn more Chinese. Gradually language came to represent our two or more opposing sets of values. If I asserted my individuality, wanted to go out with my friends, had opinions of my own, or disagreed with their plans for me, I was accused of becoming too smart for my own good now that I had grown wings. "*Cheun neuih,* stupid girl. Don't think you're better than your parents just because you know more English. You don't know anything! We've eaten more salt than you've eaten rice." Everything I heard in Chinese was a dictate. It was always one more thing I wasn't supposed to do or be, one more way I wasn't supposed to think. At school I felt stupid for not knowing the language. At home I was under attack for my rebellious views. The situation became intolerable after I came out to my parents as a lesbian.

When I ran away from home at sixteen, I sought refuge in the women's community working part-time at a feminist bookstore. I felt like I had no family, no home, no identity or culture I could claim. In between hiding from my parents and crashing at various women's houses, I hung out in the Mission playing pool with other young dykes, got high, or took to the streets when I felt like I was going to explode. Sometimes at night I found myself sitting at the counter of some greasy spoon Chinese restaurant longing for a home-cooked meal. I was lonely for someone to talk to who could understand how I felt, but I didn't even have the words to communicate what I felt.

At the bookstore, I was discovering a whole other world: women, dykes, feminists, authors, political activists, artists—people who read and talked about what they were reading. As exciting as it all was, I didn't understand what people were talking about. What was political theory? What was literary criticism? Words flew over my head like planes over a runway. In order to communicate with other feminists, most of whom were white or middle class or both, educated, and at least ten years older than me, I had to learn feminist rhetoric.

Given my uprooted and transplanted state, I have a difficult time explaining to other people how I feel about language. Usually they don't understand or will even dispute what I'm saying. A lot of times I'll think it's because I don't have the right words, I haven't read enough books, or I don't know the language. That's how I felt all the time while working at a feminist bookstore. It wasn't only white, educated people who didn't understand how I felt. Women of color or Third World women who had class privilege and came from literary backgrounds thought the problem was more my age and my lack of political development. I often felt beaten down by these kinds of attitudes while still thinking that my not being understood was the result of my inability to communicate rather than an unreceptive environment.

. . .

I knew that I needed to go some place where some of my experiences with language would be mirrored. Through the Refugee Women's Program in the Tenderloin district of San Francisco, I started to tutor two Cambodian refugee girls. The Buth family had been in the U.S. for one and a half years. They lived, twelve people to a room, in an apartment building on Eddy Street half a block from the porno theaters. I went to their home one evening a week and on Sundays took the girls to the children's library. The doorbells in the building were out of order, so visitors had to wait to be let in by someone on their way out. Often I stood on their doorsteps watching the street life. The fragrant smell of jasmine rice wafting from the windows of the apartment building mixed with the smell of booze and piss on the street. Newspapers, candy wrappers and all kinds of garbage swept up by the wind colored the sidewalks. Cars honked and sped past while Asian, Black and White kids played up and down the street. Mothers carrying their babies weaved through loose gatherings of drunk men and prostitutes near the corner store. Around me I heard a medley of languages: Vietnamese, Chinese, Cambodian, English, Black English, Laotian.

Sometimes, I arrived to find Yan and Eng sitting on the steps behind the security gate waiting to let me in. Some days they wore their school clothes, while on other days they were barefooted and wore their traditional sarongs. As we climbed the stairs up to their apartment, we inhaled fish sauce and curry and rice. Six-year-old Eng would chatter and giggle but Yan was quieter and more reserved. Although she was only eight years old, I couldn't help but feel like I was in the company of a serious adult. I immediately identified with her. I noticed how, whenever I gave them something to do, they didn't want to do it on their own. For example, they often got excited when I brought them books, but they wouldn't want to read by themselves. They became quiet and withdrawn when I asked them questions. Their answer was always a timid "I don't know," and they never asked a question or made a request. So I read with them. We did everything together. I didn't want them to feel like they were supposed to automatically know what to do, because I remembered how badly that used to make me feel.

Play time was the best part of our time together. All the little kids joined in and sometimes even their older brothers. Everybody was so excited that they forgot they were learning English. As we played jigsaw sentences and word concentration and chickens and whales, I became a little kid again, except this time I wasn't alone and unhappy. When they made Mother's Day cards, I made a Mother's Day card. When they drew pictures of our field trip to the beach, I sketched pictures of us at the beach. When we made origami frogs and jumped them all over the floor, I went home and made dinosaurs, kangaroos, spiders, crabs and lobsters. Week after week, I added to my repertoire until I could feel that little kid who used to sit like the piece of unmolded clay in front of her in art class turn into a wide-eyed origami enthusiast.

As we studied and played in the middle of the room surrounded by the rest of the family who were sleeping, nursing, doing homework, playing cards, talking, laughing or crying, Yah would frequently interrupt our lesson to answer her mother. Sometimes it was a long conversation, but I didn't mind because English was their second language. They spoke only Cambodian with their family. If they laughed at something on television, it was usually at the picture and not at the dialogue. English was used for schoolwork and to talk to me. They did not try to express their thoughts and feelings in English. When they spoke to each other, they were not alone or isolated. Whether they were living in a refugee camp in the Philippines or in Thailand or in a one-room apartment on Eddy Street, they were connected to each other through their language and their culture. They had survived war, losing family members, their country and their home, but in speaking their language, they were able to love and comfort each other. Sitting there on the bamboo mat next to the little girls, Eng and her younger sister Oeun, listening to their sweet little voices talking and singing, I understood for the first time what it was like to be a child with a voice and it made me remember my first love, the Chinese language.

While searching for an address, I came across a postcard of the San Francisco-Oakland Bay Bridge. I immediately recognized it as the postcard I had sent to my schoolmate in Hong Kong when I first got here. On the back was my eight-and-a-half-year-old handwriting.

In English it says:

> Dear Kam Yee, I received your letter. You asked if I've been to school yet. Yes, I've already found a school. My family has decided to stay in America. My living surroundings are very nice. Please don't worry about me. I'm sorry it has taken so long for me to return your letter. Okay lets talk some more next time. Please give my regards to your parents and your family. I wish you hap piness. Signed: Your classmate, Yuen Kit, August 30th.

. . .

The card, stamped "Return To Sender," is postmarked 1970. Although I have sketchy memories of my early school days in Hong Kong, I still remember the day when Kam Yee and I found each other. The bell rang signaling the end of class. Sitting up straight in our chairs, we had recited "Goodbye, teacher" in a chorus. While the others were rushing out the door to their next class, I rose from my desk and slowly put away my books. Over my left shoulder I saw Kam Yee watching me. We smiled at each other as I walked over to her desk. I had finally made a friend. Soon after that my family left Hong Kong and I wrote my last Chinese letter.

All the time that I was feeling stupid and overwhelmed by language, could I have been having the Chinese blues? By the time I was seven, I was reading the Chinese newspaper. I remember because there were a lot of reports of raped and mutilated women's bodies found in plastic bags on the side of quiet roads. It was a thrill when my father would send me to the newsstand on the corner to get his newspaper. Passing street vendors peddling sweets and fruit, I would run as quickly as I could. From a block away I could smell the stinky odor of *dauh fuh fa*, my favorite snack of slippery, warm, soft tofu in sweet syrup.

Up until a year ago, I could only recognize some of the Chinese characters on store signs, restaurant menus and Chinese newspapers on Stockton and Power Streets, but I always felt a tingle of excitement whenever I recognized a word or knew its sound, like oil sizzling in a wok just waiting for something to fry.

On Saturdays I sit with my Chinese language teacher on one of the stone benches lining the overpass where the financial district meets Chinatown and links Portsmouth Square to the Holiday Inn Hotel. We have been meeting once a week for me to practice speaking, reading and writing Chinese using whatever material we can find. Sometimes I read a bilingual Chinese American weekly newspaper called the East West Journal, other times Chinese folk tales for young readers from the Chinatown Children's Library, or bilingual brochures describing free services offered by non-profit Chinatown community agencies, and sometimes even Chinese translations of Pacific Bell Telephone inserts. I look forward to these sessions where I reach inward to recover all those lost sounds that once were the roots of my childhood imagination. This exercise in trying to use my eight-year-old vocabulary to verbalize my thoughts as an adult is as scary as it is exhilarating. At one time Chinese was poetry to me. Words, their sounds and their rhythms, conjured up images that pulled me in and gave me a physical sense of their meanings. The Chinese characters that I wrote and practiced were pictographs of water, grass, birds, fire, heart and mouth. With my calligraphy brush made of pig's hair, I made the rain fall and the wind blow.

Now, speaking Chinese with my father is the closest I have felt to coming home. In a thin but sage-like voice, he reflects on a lifetime of hard work and broken dreams and we slowly reconnect as father and daughter. As we sit across the kitchen table from one another, his old and tattered Chinese dictionary by his side, he tells me of the loving relationship he had with his mother, who encouraged him in his interest in writing and the movies. Although our immigrant experiences are generations apart and have been impacted differently by American culture, in his words I see the core of who I am. I cannot express my feelings fully in either Chinese or English or make him understand my choices. Though I am still grappling with accepting the enormous love behind the sacrifices he has made to give me a better life, I realize that with my ability to move in two different worlds I am the fruit of his labor.

For 85 cents, I can have unlimited refills of tea and a *gai mei baau* at The Sweet Fragrance Cafe on Broadway across from the World Theatre. After the first bite, the coconut sugar and butter ooze down my palm. Behind the pastry counter, my favorite clerk is consolidating trays of walnut cupcakes. Pointing to some round fried bread covered with sesame seeds, she urges the customer with "Four for a dollar, very fresh!"

Whole families from grandparents to babies sleeping soundly on mothers' backs come here for porridge, pastries and coffee. Mothers stroll in to get sweets for little ones waiting at home. Old women carrying their own mugs from home come in to chat with their buddies. Workers wearing aprons smeared with pig's blood or fresh fish scales drop in for a bite during their break. Chinese husbands sit for hours complaining and gossiping not unlike the old women in the park.

A waitress brings bowls of beef stew noodles and pork liver porridge. Smokers snub out their cigarettes as they pick up their chopsticks. The man across from me is counting sons and daughters on the fingers of his left hand:

one son, another son, my wife, one daughter. He must have family in China waiting to immigrate.

The regulars congregate at the back tables, shouting opinions from one end of the long table to the other. The Chinese are notorious for their loud conversations at close range that can easily be mistaken for arguments and fights until someone breaks into laughter or gives his companion a friendly punch. Here the drama of life is always unfolding in all different dialects. I may not understand a lot of it, but the chuckling, the hand gestures, the raising of voices in protest and in accusation, and the laughter all flow like music, like a Cantonese opera.

Twenty years seems like a long time, but it has taken all twenty years for me to understand my language blocks and to find ways to help myself learn. I have had to create my own literacy program. I had to recognize that the school system failed to meet my needs as an immigrant and that this society and its institutions doesn't reflect or validate my experiences. I have to let myself grieve over the loss of my native language and all the years wasted in classrooms staring into space or dozing off when I was feeling depressed and hopeless. My various activities now help to remind me that my relationship with language is more complex than just speaking enough English to get by. In creative activity and in anything that requires words, I'm still eight years old. Sometimes I open a book and I still feel I can't read. It may take days or weeks for me to work up the nerve to open that book again. But I do open it and it gets a little easier each time that I work through the fear. As long as there are bakeries in Chinatown and as long as I have 85 cents, I know I have a way back to myself.

QUESTIONS FOR DISCUSSION AND ANALYSIS

Historically and Geographically/Globally Contextual

1. What historical factors were instrumental in encouraging Kit's family's immigration?
2. How is Kit affected by feminism as she grows up in the 1970s and 1980s? Discuss the reasons Kit may face difficulties relating to feminists at the bookstore during this time period.
3. Kit's parents work when they enter the United States, but Kit does not disclose the type of work they do. Based on the history of Asian immigrants in the United States, speculate on what types of work they would most likely do.
4. How does the "cultural clash" between immigrant generations manifest in Kit's relationship with her parents?
5. Why does Kit forget how to think, speak, and write in Chinese? What structures of oppression and privilege make her forgetting almost inevitable?

6. Discuss recent debates over bilingual education and English in California schools. How have outcomes of this debate possibly affected Kit and Asian immigrants like her? How have these language debates affected Mexican immigrants and even African Americans in U.S. schools?
7. Kit mentions that many of her friends are "dykes." How is Kit's story reflective of broader trends in gay and lesbian movements in the 1970s and 1980s?
8. Kit works to relearn Chinese. Why might this be more acceptable today in the U.S. than 20 or 30 years ago?

Socially Constructed

9. What is the "Chinese American Dream" and how does it affect Kit and her father differently? According to this dream, who is successful and how does the Chinese American Dream compare to the ideology of the "American Dream"?
10. Why does Kit decide to relearn Chinese? How does language shape her identity and self-esteem?
11. What are the social forces in Kit's life that support her personal development and social mobility? What forces pose obstacles to her development?
12. What is the relationship between Kit's sexuality and the "Chinese American Dream"?
13. What does Kit's story tell us about American culture and the ways that immigrant families are incorporated into it?

Power Relationships

14. Discuss the various ways in which Kit challenges the power relations of race, class, gender, and sexuality that constrain her. Are her challenges successful?
15. Why did Kit's parents place their hopes for success in the fulfillment of their dreams for their children rather than in their dreams for themselves? Why did the parents feel they were powerless to resist the discrimination and racism they faced at work, on the bus, and at the supermarket?
16. How does Kit's social class influence her personal and social power?
17. How does language figure into power relations?
18. In what ways will Kit's rejuvenated interest in Chinese culture put her at a disadvantage in the United States? In what ways will it benefit her?
19. Who benefits from the existence of a "Chinese American Dream"?

Macro/Social Structural and Micro/Social Psychological Levels

20. How does language operate both as a social institution and as a means of personal empowerment in Kit's life?

21. What institutional structures work to support Kit's developing sexual orientation and racial ethnic and gender identity?
22. How does being educated in the United States affect Kit's life? Discuss some of the social costs and benefits for Kit and other Asian Americans.
23. In tutoring Yan and Eng in English, how is Kit challenging oppression?
24. From what we know about Kit's life, how does American culture differ from Chinese culture? How do these cultural differences affect Kit's daily experience?
25. What evidence is there that Kit has internalized society's negative views of people like her?
26. Is language both a macro-level institution and a micro-level tool?

Simultaneously Expressed

27. How do Kit and her family simultaneously experience systems of race, class, gender, and sexuality in their lives?
28. Kit seems unable to bridge the gap between American culture and Chinese culture for most of her life. How do constructions of race, class, gender, and sexuality contribute to the gap?
29. How does the refugee status of the Buth family affect their lives?
30. What oppressions seem to be the most prominent in Kit's life? Are other forces of oppression obscured?
31. How might Kit's oppression have been different if she had been born in the United States? If she had come to the U.S. only for college?
32. How do you think Kit's brother will fare in life, compared to her? Will he be better off? Do you think he may have an easier adjustment to American culture? Why or why not?

Implications for Social Action and Social Justice

33. How can Kit's story contribute to the search for social justice for all immigrant groups?
34. What implications does Kit's story have for American educational policy?
35. Who is Kit's audience? Other Asian immigrant women like herself? Feminists? Her family? Someone else? What is her main message to this audience?
36. How might Kit's teachers, acquaintances, and family react to her story? What implications do their reactions have for social activism?
37. Kit's story is partly about self-definition and self-valuation. How is this an important strategy for resisting oppression?

REFERENCES

Ancheta, Angelo N. 1998. *Race, Rights, and the Asian American Experience*. New Brunswick, NJ: Rutgers University Press.

Anzaldúa, Gloria (Ed.). 1990. *Making Face, Making Soul, Haciendo Caras: Creative and Critical Perspectives by Feminists of Color.* San Francisco: Aunt Lute Foundation Books.

Ng, Franklin (Ed.). 1998. *Asians in America: The Peoples of East, Southeast, and South Asia in American Life and Culture.* Volumes 1–6. New York: Garland Publishing, Inc.

Okhiro, Gary Y., Marilyn Alquizola, Dorothy Fujita Rony, and K. Scott Wang (Eds.). 1995. *Privileging Positions: The Sites of Asian American Studies.* Pullman, WA: Washington State University Press.

Shah, Sonia. 1997. *Dragon Ladies: Asian American Feminists Breathe Fire.* Boston: South End Press.

Takaki, Ronald T. 1998. *Strangers from a Different Shore: A History of Asian Americans Revised.* Boston, MA: Little, Brown & Co.

Man Child: A Black Lesbian Feminist's Response[1]

Audre Lorde

This article is not a theoretical discussion of Lesbian Mothers and their Sons, nor a how-to article. It is an attempt to scrutinize and share some pieces of that common history belonging to my son and me. I have two children: a fifteen-and-a-half-year-old daughter Beth, and a fourteen-year-old son Jonathan. This is the way it was/is with me and Jonathan, and I leave the theory to another time and person. This is one woman's telling.

I have no golden message about the raising of sons for other lesbian mothers, no secret to transpose your questions into certain light. I have my own ways of rewording those same questions, hoping we will all come to speak those questions and pieces of our lives we need to share. We are women making contact within ourselves and with each other across the restrictions of a printed page, bent upon the use of our own/one another's knowledges.

The truest direction comes from inside. I give the most strength to my children by being willing to look within myself, and by being honest with them about what I find there, without expecting a response beyond their years. In this way they begin to learn to look beyond their own fears.

All our children are outriders for a queendom not yet assured.

My adolescent son's growing sexuality is a conscious dynamic between Jonathan and me. It would be presumptuous of me to discuss Jonathan's sexuality here, except to state my belief that whomever he chooses to explore this area with, his choices will be nonoppressive, joyful, and deeply felt from within, places of growth.

One of the difficulties in writing this piece has been temporal; this is the summer when Jonathan is becoming a man, physically. And our sons must become men—such men as we hope our daughters, born and unborn, will be pleased to live among. Our sons will not grow into women. Their way is more difficult than that of our daughters, for they must move away from us, without us. Hopefully, our sons have what they have learned from us, and a howness to forge it into their own image.

Our daughters have us, for measure or rebellion or outline or dream; but the sons of lesbians have to make their own definitions of self as men. This is both power and vulnerability. The sons of lesbians have the advantage of our blueprints for survival, but they must take what we know and transpose it into their own maleness. May the goddess be kind to my son, Jonathan.

Recently I have met young Black men about whom I am pleased to say that their future and their visions, as well as their concerns within the present, intersect more closely with Jonathan's than do my own. I have shared vision with these men as well as temporal strategies for our survivals and I appreciate the spaces in which we could sit down together. Some of these men I met at the First Annual Conference of Third World Lesbians and Gays held in Washington D.C. in October, 1979. I have met others in different places and do not know how they identify themselves sexually. Some of these men are raising families alone. Some have adopted sons. They are Black men who dream and who act and who own their feelings, questioning. It is heartening to know our sons do not step out alone.

When Jonathan makes me angriest, I always say he is bringing out the testosterone in me. What I mean is that he is representing some piece of myself as a woman that I am reluctant to acknowledge or explore. For instance, what does "acting like a man" mean? For me, what I reject? For Jonathan, what he is trying to redefine?

Raising Black children—female and male—in the mouth of a racist, sexist, suicidal dragon is perilous and chancy. If they cannot love and resist at the same time, they will probably not survive. And in order to survive they must let go. This is what mothers teach—love, survival—that is, self-definition and letting go. For each of these, the ability to feel strongly and to recognize those feelings is central: how to feel love, how to neither discount fear nor be overwhelmed by it, how to enjoy feeling deeply.

I wish to raise a Black man who will not be destroyed by, nor settle for, those corruptions called *power* by the White fathers who mean his destruction as surely as they mean mine. I wish to raise a Black man who will recognize that the legitimate objects of his hostility are not women, but the particulars of a structure that programs him to fear and despise women as well as his own Black self.

For me, this task begins with teaching my son that I do not exist to do his feeling for him.

Men who are afraid to feel must keep women around to do their feeling for them while dismissing us for the same supposedly "inferior" capacity to feel deeply. But in this way also, men deny themselves their own essential humanity, becoming trapped in dependency and fear.

As a Black woman committed to a liveable future, and as a mother loving and raising a boy who will become a man, I must examine all my possibilities of being within such a destructive system.

Jonathan was three-and-one-half when Frances, my lover, and I met; he was seven when we all began to live together permanently. From the start, Frances' and my insistence that there be no secrets in our household about the fact that we were lesbians has been the source of problems and strengths for both children. In the beginning, this insistence grew out of the knowledge, on both our parts, that whatever was hidden out of fear could always be used either against the children or ourselves—one imperfect but useful argument for honesty. The knowledge of fear can help make us free.

> for the embattled
> there is no place
> that cannot be
> home
> nor is.[2]

For survival, Black children in America must be raised to be warriors. For survival, they must also be raised to recognize the enemy's many faces. Black children of lesbian couples have an advantage because they learn, very early, that oppression comes in many different forms, none of which have anything to do with their own worth.

To help give me perspective, I remember that for years, in the namecalling at school, boys shouted at Jonathan not—"your mother's a lesbian"—but rather—"your mother's a nigger."

When Jonathan was eight years old and in the third grade we moved, and he went to a new school where his life was hellish as a new boy on the block. He did not like to play rough games. He did not like to fight. He did not like to stone dogs. And all this marked him early on as an easy target.

When he came in crying one afternoon, I heard from Beth how the corner bullies were making Jonathan wipe their shoes on the way home whenever Beth wasn't there to fight them off. And when I heard that the ringleader was a little boy in Jonathan's class his own size, an interesting and very disturbing thing happened to me.

My fury at my own long-ago impotence, and my present pain at his suffering, made me start to forget all that I knew about violence and fear, and blaming the victim, I started to hiss at the weeping child. "The next time you come in here crying . . . ," and I suddenly caught myself in horror.

This is the way we allow the destruction of our sons to begin—in the name of protection and to ease our own pain. *My* son get beaten up? I was about to demand that he buy that first lesson in the corruption of power, that might makes right. I could hear myself beginning to perpetuate the age-old distortions about what strength and bravery really are.

And no, Jonathan didn't have to fight if he didn't want to, but somehow he did have to feel better about not fighting. An old horror rolled over me of being the fat kid who ran away, terrified of getting her glasses broken.

About that time a very wise woman said to me, "Have you ever told Jonathan that once you used to be afraid, too?"

The idea seemed far-out to me at the time, but the next time he came in crying and sweaty from having run away again, I could see that he felt shamed at having failed me, or some image he and I had created in his head of mother/woman. This image of woman being able to handle it all was bolstered by the fact that he lived in a household with three strong women, his lesbian parents and his forthright older sister. At home, for Jonathan, power was clearly female.

[2]Audre Lorde, excerpt from "School Note" from *The Black Unicorn*. Copyright © 1978 by Audre Lorde. Reprinted with the permission of W. W. Norton & Company, Inc.

And because our society teaches us to think in an either/or mode—kill or be killed, dominate or be dominated—this meant that he must either surpass or be lacking. I could see the implications of this line of thought. Consider the two western classic myth/models of mother/son relationships: Jocasta/Oedipus, the son who fucks his mother, and Clytemnestra/Orestes, the son who kills his mother.

It all felt connected to me.

I sat down on the hallway steps and took Jonathan on my lap and wiped his tears. "Did I ever tell you about how I used to be afraid when I was your age?"

I will never forget the look on that little boy's face as I told him the tale of my glasses and my after-school fights. It was a look of relief and total disbelief, all rolled into one.

It is as hard for our children to believe that we are not omnipotent as it is for us to know it, as parents. But that knowledge is necessary as the first step in the reassessment of power as something other than might, age, privilege, or the lack of fear. It is an important step for a boy, whose societal destruction begins when he is forced to believe that he can only be strong if he doesn't feel, or if he wins.

I thought about all this one year later when Beth and Jonathan, ten and nine, were asked by an interviewer how they thought they had been affected by being children of a feminist.

Jonathan said that he didn't think there was too much in feminism for boys, although it certainly was good to be able to cry if he felt like it and not to have to play football if he didn't want to. I think of this sometimes now when I see him practicing for his Brown Belt in Tai Kwon Do.

The strongest lesson I can teach my son is the same lesson I teach my daughter: how to be who he wishes to be for himself. And the best way I can do this is to be who I am and hope that he will learn from this not how to be me, which is not possible, but how to be himself. And this means how to move to that voice from within himself, rather than to those raucous, persuasive, or threatening voices from outside, pressuring him to be what the world wants him to be.

And that is hard enough.

Jonathan is learning to find within himself some of the different faces of courage and strength, whatever he chooses to call them. Two years ago, when Jonathan was twelve and in the seventh grade, one of his friends at school who had been to the house persisted in calling Frances "the maid." When Jonathan corrected him, the boy then referred to her as "the cleaning woman." Finally Jonathan said, simply, "Frances is not the cleaning women, she's my mother's lover." Interestingly enough, it is the teachers at this school who still have not recovered from his openness.

Frances and I were considering attending a Lesbian/Feminist conference this summer, when we were notified that no boys over ten were allowed. This presented logistic as well as philosophical problems for us, and we sent the following letter:

Sisters:

Ten years as an interracial lesbian couple has taught us both the dangers of an oversimplified approach to the nature and solutions of any oppression, as well as the danger inherent in an incomplete vision.

Our thirteen-year-old son represents as much hope for our future world as does our fifteen-year-old daughter, and we are not willing to abandon him to the killing streets of New York City while we journey west to help form a Lesbian-Feminist vision of the future world in which we can all survive and flourish. I hope we can continue this dialogue in the near future, as I feel it is important to our vision and our survival.

The question of separatism is by no means simple. I am thankful that one of my children is male, since that helps to keep me honest. Every line I write shrieks there are no easy solutions.

I grew up in largely female environments, and I know how crucial that has been to my own development. I feel the want and need often for the society of women, exclusively. I recognize that our own spaces are essential for developing and recharging.

As a Black woman, I find it necessary to withdraw into all-Black groups at times for exactly the same reasons—differences in stages of development and differences in levels of interaction. Frequently, when speaking with men and White women, I am reminded of how difficult and time-consuming it is to have to reinvent the pencil every time you want to send a message.

But this does not mean that my responsibility for my son's education stops at age ten, any more than it does for my daughter's. However, for each of them, that responsibility does grow less and less as they become more woman and man.

Both Beth and Jonathan need to know what they can share and what they cannot, how they are joined and how they are not. And Frances and I, as grown women and lesbians coming more and more into our power, need to relearn the experience that difference does not have to be threatening.

When I envision the future, I think of the world I crave for my daughters and my sons. It is thinking for survival of the species—thinking for life.

Most likely there will always be women who move with women, women who live with men, men who choose men. I work for a time when women with women, women with men, men with men, all share the work of a world that does not barter bread or self for obedience, nor beauty, nor love. And in that world we will raise our children free to choose how best to fulfill themselves. For we are jointly responsible for the care and raising of the young, since *that* they be raised is a function, ultimately, of the species.

Within that tripartite pattern of relating/existence, the raising of the young will be the joint responsibility of all adults who choose to be associated with children. Obviously, the children raised within each of these three relationships will be different, lending a special savor to that eternal inquiry into how best can we live our lives.

Jonathan was three-and-a-half when Frances and I met. He is now fourteen years old. I feel the living perspective that having lesbian parents has brought to Jonathan is a valuable addition to his human sensitivity.

Jonathan has had the advantage of growing up within a nonsexist relationship, one in which this society's pseudonatural assumptions of ruler/
ruled are being challenged. And this is not only because Frances and I are lesbians, for unfortunately there are some lesbians who are still locked into patri-
archal patterns of unequal power relationships.

These assumptions of power relationships are being questioned because
Frances and I, often painfully and with varying degrees of success, attempt to
evaluate and measure over and over again our feelings concerning power, our
own and others'. And we explore with care those areas concerning how it is
used and expressed between us and between us and the children, openly and
otherwise. A good part of our biweekly family meetings are devoted to this
exploration.

As parents, Frances and I have given Jonathan our love, our openness, and
our dreams to help form his visions. Most importantly, as the son of lesbians,
he has had an invaluable model—not only of a relationship—but of relating.

Jonathan is fourteen now. In talking over this paper with him and asking
his permission to share some pieces of his life, I asked Jonathan what he felt
were the strongest negative and the strongest positive aspects for him in having grown up with lesbian parents.

He said the strongest benefit he felt he had gained was that he knew a lot
more about people than most other kids his age that he knew, and that he did
not have a lot of the hang-ups that some other boys did about men and women.

And the most negative aspect he felt, Jonathan said, was the ridicule he
got from some kids with straight parents.

"You mean, from your peers?" I said.

"Oh no," he answered promptly. "My peers know better. I mean other kids."

QUESTIONS FOR DISCUSSION AND ANALYSIS

Historically and Geographically/Globally Contextual

1. Lorde states that she and Frances are finally coming into their own power
   as lesbian parents. What historical movements have contributed to their
   ability to do this?
2. How have notions of family changed over time in the United States? What
   forms of families are now and have been legally sanctioned?
3. How might Lorde and her family be affected by the contemporary "family
   values" debates? How might they also affect the debates?
4. Lorde discusses the difficulties of raising her son in an unequal, discrimi-
   natory world in 1979. How might her experience be different if she were
   writing today? In what ways might it be easier for Lorde to raise a teenage
   Black son? In what ways might it be more difficult?

5. Families headed by females and lesbian couples are more common now than in 1979. How does this change our perception of Lorde's story?

Socially Constructed

6. What are the social forces in Jonathan's life that operate to support his personal development and social mobility? What forces operate against him?
7. Why was it important for Jonathan to know that his mother has been afraid too? How did he perceive her before? What societal images of Black women likely contributed to his perception?
8. Jonathan says the strongest benefit of growing up with lesbian parents is understanding more about people than most teenagers. What does he mean? How are his ideas different from other teenagers'?
9. The organizers of the lesbian-feminist conference denied entrance to Jonathan. Why? What is gained and lost by having such a policy? What view of gender is implied by it?
10. How would this narrative be different if it were told from the perspective of Jonathan, Beth, or Frances? Are there multiple truths within the narrative? Whose?

Power Relationships

11. Lorde suggests that we like to think of things in "either/or" categories. What does she mean, and how does this relate to power?
12. How does Lorde encourage Jonathan and Beth to redefine power as something other than might or lack of fear? What are the social/political implications of this perspective?
13. In what ways does Lorde's success in raising Jonathan challenge power structures of race, class, gender, and sexuality?
14. Lorde does not mention social class as a factor in her family's life. How might we interpret this omission?
15. Why does Lorde initially have trouble with Jonathan's inability to deal with his schoolmates successfully? How does she relate to his experiences? Did she act out of internalized oppression?

Macro/Social Structural and Micro/Social Psychological Levels

16. How does Lorde define parenthood? How does this definition relate to the dominant construction of parenthood?
17. How does Jonathan confront and negotiate stereotypical images of African-American males?
18. How are race, class, gender, and sexuality power relations evident in the institutional structures that the family faces?

19. How does Lorde's family both uphold and challenge the social institution of the American family?
20. How does Lorde resist the macro structures that constrain Jonathan's development and survival? What implications do her actions have for these institutions?

Simultaneously Expressed

21. How do systems of race, class, gender, and sexuality affect Lorde's life?
22. Why does Lorde only briefly mention that she is in an interracial relationship? How are some social constructions foregrounded in her story while others remain in the background? Are these others really less important?
23. Why does Jonathan attribute the teasing and bullying he experiences to race and sexuality, rather than to gender, class, or something else?
24. How is Lorde able to shape our perceptions of which structures are important in her narrative? How would her narrative be different if she were writing about her daughter instead?
25. Why doesn't Lorde ever mention class? Consider the role of class privilege in shaping her life. How does it relate to other structures of race, gender, and sexuality within her narrative?

Implications for Social Action and Social Justice

26. Who is Lorde's audience? Other lesbians raising children? Feminists? Other Black women? All mothers? Men? Someone else? What is her message to this audience?
27. How do Lorde and her family resist oppressive structures on both individual and social levels?
28. How can Lorde's narrative contribute to the development of just family policies?
29. What advice does Jonathan offer children of lesbian parents?
30. How do Lorde's ideas help us to redefine power as something other than physical force or privilege?

REFERENCES

Baca Zinn, Maxine and Bonnie Thornton Dill (Eds.). 1994. *Women of Color in U.S. Society*. Philadelphia, PA: Temple University Press.

Bell-Scott, Patricia and Juanita Johnson-Bailey (Eds.). 1998. *Flat-Footed Truths: Telling Black Women's Lives*. 1st Edition. New York: Henry Holt.

Blasius, Mark and Shane Phelan (Eds.). 1997. *We Are Everywhere: A Historical Sourcebook of Gay and Lesbian Politics*. New York: Routledge.

Boykin, Keith. 1998. *One More River to Cross: Black and Gay in America.*
    New York: Doubleday.
Constantine-Simms, Delroy (Ed.). 2001. *The Greatest Taboo: Homosexuality in Black Communities.* Los Angeles, CA: Alyson Publications.
Lorde, Audre. 1979. "Man Child: A Black Lesbian Feminist's Response."
    Conditions 4, pp. 30–36.

CASE STUDY 7

"White Trash" and Female in a Southern Community[1]

James T. Sears

. . . Norma Jean was three years old when her mother, Eva, took a waitress job at a Christian barbecue hut. Eva scuttled her three year marriage to an army sergeant after suffering one too many drunken batterings. For the next 13 years, Eva slipped in and out of male relationships, often leaving Norma Jean and her younger brother, Roy, to fend for themselves.

A short, pugnacious girl with an oval face and a scraggly frame, Norma Jean unquestioningly followed adult orders. "I was very rule oriented. What they told me to do, I did. I did what was expected of me—nothing more. I didn't have a lot of incentives to do much more." Though she spent time talking with girls at school most of her time was spent with males. "I guess you can say I was a tomboy," recalls Norma Jean. "I played with a lot of little fellas. Since I grew up in a predominantly male environment, we'd all play football and that kind of thing."

Norma Jean does not clearly recall her childhood. A mediocre student, she looked forward to school simply because it was a way "to get out of the house. I associated being home with some of the problems that I had with my family." After school she would go home to watch television and to read school-girl romances until her bedtime. Her most serious home problem was repeated sexual abuse by her father (who would visit home occasionally), as well as by uncles, cousins, and other men who dated Eva. "I've blocked out a lot of my past because of that," Norma Jean explains. "It's still hard for me to imagine sexual intercourse happening to me at that age." Asked why she never reported this to her mother or to another adult, she replies:

> I felt like I couldn't get out of it. I couldn't say anything. Who would believe me? I was doing it to myself. I thought I was seducing those men. I thought it was *their* right. I told my mother about the incidents with my father three nights before she died. We cried together. She told me that she had been sent to reform school for running away after being raped by her stepfather and accused by her mother of lying—to get out of reform school she ended up marrying my father.

Divorced and living in a small town, Eva and her children's economic status and social reputation were marginal. Norma Jean was not a member of the "right group" at school and a day seldom passed without her little brother getting into a fight protecting the family name. Norma Jean remembers an incident at the local Southern Baptist church in which their lowly status was publicly proclaimed. "My mother had a miscarriage; she was not married. After she got back from the hospital we went to our church. The minister gave a sermon and mentioned how having babies out of wedlock was a sin. He said, 'We have one amongst us,' and pointed my mother out."

At the beginning of Norma Jean's sixth grade, Eva remarried. Norma Jean remembers:

> We were buying this house—then Eddie stepped in. He wanted to buy a new house. So, we moved out to the country and bought this house. Then it burned down. So we got a trailer and we put it out there. But, Eddie couldn't hold his job. He took money from where he was working. From then on it was downhill—I guess you could say we were poor White trash.

Norma Jean's relationship with her stepfather, Eddie, was not positive though he was one of the few adult males who never sexually abused her. "Before my mother remarried, there were different men living with her. Then Eddie stepped in. I didn't like him. I don't like him. I never will like him. I think I was also afraid of him because of the relationships with the male members in my family." Norma Jean also resented living in a rural community. "We were in the real sticks. I go down in the area even now. There's still a dirt road that washes out when it rains. We didn't know our neighbors like we did when we lived in town. All we had were trees." She spent most of her time alone playing make-believe.

Though her grades never rose above average, Norma Jean found school in the country more enjoyable than town. Since "people didn't have any predispositions of how they felt about me," she tried to associate with those outside the boundaries of her social class. "Inside my head people were in different classes, higher, lower, whatever. At school I wanted to be around the popular ingroup. These were kids who were good looking, popular, had good grades, involved in a lot of activities. These were kids whose families seemed well-off and happy. Maybe I felt it would rub off." Seeking affection and affirmation, she hung around them without any hope of becoming part of their group.

> I didn't think of myself as a very friendly person. I saw myself as short, fat, and ugly. Nobody wanted to be around me so I felt being around them I could at least get some residual affection. Not that they gave it to me but being around them I could just feel it among themselves.

Norma Jean's presence was tolerated for a brief time. Then an incident occurred.

> There was this really small girl in our class. One day I was trying to prove to somebody that I was strong. I wrapped my arms around her waist, picked her up, and carried her around the classroom. You know, little girls just don't do that. It chilled out a lot of people and my friendship circle sort of changed. I started hanging out with the next highest group. But, I was still alone in the crowd.

Norma Jean had no interest in boys during middle-school. Given her concern to be well-liked and, at least, on the periphery of a circle of friends, she participated in the daily banter among female classmates.

> When they talked about boys, I talked about boys. When they talked about doing interesting things with boys, I'd seem interested and give a lot of supportive conversation. But, I'd never commit to anything, I'd never outright lie unless it came right down to it. When they started talking about real feminine things like makeup and stuff, I'd leave because I'd feel uncomfortable.

The summer before Norma Jean entered ninth grade, Eddie abandoned the family. The family moved back to town to live in a rented trailer. Norma Jean attended a middle-class, predominantly White high school in Columbia. The next three years were more enjoyable in school because of a new found interest: junior ROTC. "I could take either PE or ROTC. I figured they're not going to make me run up and down like PE so I signed up. ROTC gave me direction. It gave me clear objectives. I could do them and excel at them—like drilling with weapons." With a sparkle in her eye, Norma Jean asked, "Would you like for me to demonstrate?" Standing up she spouted:

> The officer would step in front of you and ask, "What is the nomenclature of your rifle?" I would say, "Sir. The nomenclature is the M190383, a Springfield, lightweight, manually operated, magazine fed, brief shorter weapon, sir." I felt very good about ROTC. You can sort of tell.

During these ROTC activities Norma Jean had a place in school; there was meaning and direction for what she did. Outside of ROTC she was an "outcast." At lunch time, she associated with two other outcasts in the school cafeteria: Marty, "an obese fella who was a science fiction freak," and Hilda, "a real slight, quiet, pimply-faced girl who was into art."

Although she enjoyed ROTC, she was given a difficult time by other ROTC members.

> They were real mean toward people who were at all different. I was known as a "boy/girl" because people thought I wanted to be a boy. They said I did all the things that the boys did. I wanted to be an officer. God! Did I want to be an officer. I wanted to be on the drill team. They didn't like that. Girls didn't do stuff like that. Unlike the other girls in ROTC, I was more masculine and more rural. Nobody accepted me, my authority, or my ideas because I was a girl.

Norma Jean attempted to cross these boundaries seeking affection and identity through her association with the ROTC group which expressed little toleration or kindness to her. Trying to gain their favor, Norma Jean routinely made fun of her outcast friends, Marty and Hilda.

> It was a real paradox. How could I be friends with the people I'm making fun of? But, it's easy sometimes. I guess I made it easy. I wanted so much to be identified with the people in ROTC that I came up with jokes and lies about these people who were different. Then, I'd be friends with Marty and Hilda because they accepted me as I was and didn't make any real demands on me. But, I did my best to meet the demands of the ROTC people by making jokes so that they wouldn't look at me so much as a "boy/girl."

Norma Jean identified herself as a heterosexual person throughout adolescence. "If I had known a person who was gay, I just might have wanted to talk to her about it—without anybody seeing me. Not because I was gay but because I've never talked to anybody who was that way." Norma Jean did not begin to date, however, until the tenth grade when she would go out with Marty or Mickey, an "ROTC man." Her feelings of attraction for these boys were rather weak: "I was sexually attracted to them. I mean, it was expected that I would go out with fellas. Sometimes, I guess, I liked making out. I liked kissing. But, that was all I liked doing. So, I provided a real problem to some. I never had intercourse."

Norma Jean, however, continued to be molested by her mother's adult boyfriends. "It was very sporadic," she recalls. "I didn't bother with it. When it happened, I forgot about it—I tried to anyway." During this time, Norma Jean became interested in her physical education teacher. "I thought she was real cute. I was sort of attracted to her but I didn't admit that to myself or to others. I'd say, 'Gosh! She's an ugly bitch.' " Within Norma Jean's world, neither homosexual behavior nor identity existed: "It wasn't an option. If I felt an attraction, I'd say, 'I just want to be friendly with her,' or, 'She's just a nice friend.' Sexuality would be taken away. I wouldn't attribute my friendship to that kind of thing."

Eva died of complications associated with diabetes the summer before Norma Jean's senior year. With the death of her mother, Norma Jean and her brother, Roy, went to live with their Aunt Felicia in a rural South Carolina town. They attended a lower-class, predominantly black school:

> We were country rednecks. In that school, country rednecks would go to the big tree in the school lot to smoke cigarettes. Girls sucked face with the guys or the girls stuck together and the guys did their thing. I was very much alone. I didn't like being with those people.

Neither Roy nor she got along with their aunt. "He argued with my Aunt Felicia. Nobody argues with Aunt Felicia. Roy left for a foster family first." Two months after her mom had died, Norma Jean was living with an upper-class foster family in the same town. She remembers:

> It was a big difference. Though my aunt had money, she didn't have the attitudes. I wasn't identified with the rednecks anymore. I didn't have to go out to the tree. I got a real different image of myself. When I changed families, I could really spend time with other kinds of students. These were people of a different class. Before I wasn't friends with them but when I changed families I could really spend time with these people.

Roy's foster parents, on the other hand, were "middle class in their money but not in their attitudes." He continued to hang around the old tree occasionally harassing Norma Jean for crossing her class boundary and leaving his world behind.

As the year progressed, and with the support of her well-placed foster parents, Norma Jean concentrated on her studies and participated in a variety of school activities including the drama and math clubs. Norma Jean's move to a more academic-oriented program with better grades is partly attributable to her change in schools. As she realizes, "When a little fish in a big pond moves to a little pond the fish seems to get bigger. It really doesn't. But, being mediocre at this suburban school was excelling in this rural school." The expectations placed by her foster parents and their status within this small rural community also were important. Norma Jean remains grateful for their support:

> I just saw something in Katie as my foster mother and she must have seen something in me. She helped me a lot. At the city school, before my mother died, I was in ROTC and that was it. When I first came to this school, they didn't have an ROTC program. It broke my heart when I found out. That one year, with Katie's help, I did more than I ever did at the other school.

With her foster family's support, Norma Jean crossed over another boundary. Katie and her husband "assumed that I would go to college. It was sort of a dream when I was in high school although before my mother died it wasn't even possible." Norma Jean's dream became a reality the next year.

"When I came to college," Norma Jean recollects, "I was still doing things that were expected of me. I dated a fella and became very involved with him. I probably would have married this fella had he not been killed. I was very emotionally attached to David before he died. We were very sexually active except for penetration." Five days before his birthday, David was killed by a drunk driver as he was bicycling.

Shortly after this tragedy, Norma Jean quit college, moved in with her grandparents, and began work at a convenience store. "I was sort of wishy washy then. It was like, 'Now I am an adult. I've got to act like an adult but I don't know what to do.' So I tried to talk to people at work. I found out about this one woman, Charmaine." Norma Jean began to think about homosexuality. While working at the store, she became more conscious of her sexual feelings toward women. She recalls:

> Some women runners kept coming by the store where I was. After they finished practicing, all of these gorgeous bodies would just pile into the store to get something to drink. I became very sexually excited about that. I made sure that I worked the nights they practiced.

Norma Jean also began thinking about Charmaine in a sexual way.

> I had this real strong image of her being gay. I couldn't ask her. You don't ask people outright, "Are you gay?" So, I had to think of a story: One of my best friends told me that her roommate used to think that she was gay. Her roommate would leave the room and never change clothes in front of her. I asked, "Well, Charmaine how should I act? My best friend just told me that her roommate used to think she was gay. Damn! I think she is gay. How am I suppose to act?" Charmaine said to me, "What's different?" I said, "Well, she is gay now." She asked me, "What's changed about her?" I just kept saying, "She's gay." Charmaine said, "Well, nothing has really changed. You just know one more thing about her." So, I spent a lot of time with Charmaine.

As their relationship grew closer, Charmaine introduced Norma Jean to her roommate, Eloise. One evening she accompanied the two to a gay bar. "I hyper-ventilated the whole time I was there," recollects Norma Jean. For the next two months, she continued to accompany the two though "I had a hard time adjusting to thinking about being gay." Finally, she ventured out alone:

> I wanted to find out what sex was like. One night I got drunk and proposi-tioned three women. I went to a motel with the third one. I had my first expe-rience of sex. I was real turned on. It was like, "This is it!" I felt really good about it. With women I felt I could express myself better and more freely.

Three days later Norma Jean moved in with the third woman and her lover moved out. Two months later they had broken up. Within that year, Norma Jean had moved into six different places and had four lovers. Through-out this time, Norma Jean continued to visit with Charmaine and her room-mate, Eloise. Norma Jean and Eloise grew closer as they explored their differ-ent social histories which so strangely intersected. Eloise, a fiery red-head with a quick wit, is a refined product of generations of social grooming. Eloise was everything Norma Jean was not: feminine in appearance, schooled in private all-girls academies, born to a family whose ancestors were among the founders of Charleston. Despite or perhaps because of their differences, they became lovers, a relationship that has blossomed for more than a year. Norma Jean reflects on their 16 months together:

> Eloise is a good friend. We talk about a lot of different things. We usually do all the things we can together except during school hours. We go to the bar five or six times a month. We regularly attend the gay meetings on campus as well as a women's group which is not homosexual in its orientation.

Eloise is completing her graduate degree in journalism while Norma Jean plans to become a social worker after finishing college, because, as she puts it, "I have a real identification with lower socio-economic people."

. . .

QUESTIONS FOR DISCUSSION AND ANALYSIS

Historically and Geographically/Globally Contextual

1. In what ways was Norma Jean's life experience particularly Southern? How might her life have been different had she grown up in another rural area in the United States? What historical patterns of race, class, gender, and sexuality in the southern United States are manifest in Norma Jean's story?

2. How was Norma Jean's life affected by the women's movement and the gay rights movement? How would her life have been different had she

grown up in the 1950s? Would she have followed her sexual preferences for women? Would she have been involved in ROTC?

3. Why weren't Norma Jean and Roy adopted? Consider the contemporary context of adoption and foster care in the United States. Why might Norma Jean and Roy have had foster care rather than adoption experiences?

4. How were Norma Jean and her mother influenced by similar structures of oppression and privilege? What has changed over time for women in the rural South?

Socially Constructed

5. Trace the different types of family configurations Norma Jean experiences throughout her life. How could Norma Jean's experiences uphold or challenge current "family values" debates?

6. In what ways does Norma Jean's story both challenge and reinforce the American Dream ideology?

7. Norma Jean's brother is constantly getting in fights to "protect the family name." How does Norma Jean's concept of family differ from her brother's? Why does he harass her for "leaving his world behind"?

8. Norma Jean repeatedly refers to herself as a boy/girl. Does she view this image as positive or negative? How did individuals and institutions help to shape this self-concept?

9. Norma Jean states that homosexuality did not exist in her adolescent world. Why is this important for understanding the construction of sexuality? How did her life change when she was able to label her feelings?

10. Throughout her life, Norma Jean changes social class, racial contexts, and rural-urban contexts. Consider how these shifts affected her view of herself, her involvements, her relationships.

Power Relationships

11. Who benefits from the foster care system? Children like Norma Jean and Roy? Their biological family members? The foster care/adoption families? The government or foster care workers?

12. Why did members of ROTC refuse to accept Norma Jean's authority as an officer? How did this refusal shape her understanding of power?

13. How does Norma Jean resist various power structures of race, class, gender, and sexuality?

14. Throughout her story there is evidence that Norma Jean has internalized society's negative images of people like her—Southerners, working-class Whites, masculine girls, lesbians, rural folk. How do these internalizations limit her life?

15. What do Norma Jean's "class crossover" experiences tell us about class oppression and power relationships?

Macro/Social Structural and Micro/Social Psychological Levels

16. What types of controlling images or stereotypes does Norma Jean confront? How does she negotiate these images?
17. Norma Jean mentions that being mediocre in a suburban school means excelling in a rural school. How did this affect her self-concept? What does her story tell us about the role of schools in producing race, class, gender, and sexuality inequality?
18. Norma Jean mentions that as a little girl she was "rule oriented." How could this be analyzed in terms of the larger structure of class?
19. What does Norma Jean's narrative suggest about the importance of parents in shaping children's lives? What about the influence of other adults? In what ways are race, class, gender, and sexuality systems shaped in family life?
20. In what ways does the institution of religion produce or challenge hierarchies of race, class, gender, and sexuality in this story?
21. The only jobs mentioned are jobs that women in this story held: waitress, convenience store clerk, social worker, and journalist. What kinds of jobs are these? Why do the women in this story hold these jobs? Why don't we hear about men's jobs?

Simultaneously Expressed

22. How have race, class, gender, and sexuality hierarchies affected Norma Jean's and her brother's lives differently?
23. Norma Jean refers to her family as "White trash." What role does this construct play in promoting systems of race and class privilege? If you are considered "White trash," do you have race privilege?
24. Norma Jean discusses both sexuality and class as major sites of oppression in her life, yet she does not make connections between them. How are class and sexuality interrelated in Norma Jean's life?
25. Norma Jean does not discuss gender as a major source of her oppression, yet gender and sexuality are explicitly linked. What can we learn from Norma Jean's omission of this system?
26. What structures of oppression or privilege seem least important in Norma Jean's life? Why? If we focused on only one site of oppression or privilege, what would we be missing from Norma Jean's narrative?

Implications for Social Action and Social Justice

27. If Norma Jean had been active in the women's or gay rights movements, how would her life have been different?
28. How does Norma Jean's decision to become a social worker relate to her own experience?

29. What can we learn about interlocking systems of oppression from Norma Jean's story?
30. How could Norma Jean's story be used to support or challenge the current foster care and adoption system?
31. In what ways might your analyses of Norma Jean's life support positive social change? Could they be used to reinforce existing ideologies and structures of oppression?

REFERENCES

Clendinen, Dudley. 1999. *Out for Good: The Struggle to Build a Gay Rights Movement in America.* New York: Simon and Schuster.

D'Emilio, John. 1998. *Sexual Politics, Sexual Communities: The Making of a Homosexual Minority in the United States, 1940–1970.* 2nd Edition. Chicago: University of Chicago Press.

Howard, John (Ed.). 1997. *Carryin' On in the Lesbian and Gay South.* New York: New York University Press.

Sears, James T. 1997. *Lonely Hunters: An Oral History of Lesbian and Gay Southern Life, 1948–1968.* Boulder, CO: Westview Press.

———— 1991. *Growing Up Gay in the South: Race, Gender, and Journeys of the Spirit.* New York: Harrington Park Press.

Wray, Matt and Annalee Newitz (Eds.). 1997. *White Trash: Race and Class in America.* New York: Routledge.

The Valenzuela Family[1]

Leo R. Chavez

Beatriz and Enrique Valenzuela live southeast of downtown San Diego. Their two-bedroom house is on a street lined with other modest, single-family homes in an older, relatively low-income neighborhood. A block away runs a major avenue, along which the walls of some buildings are covered with graffiti. As we sat in their living room sipping on sodas, they talked about their lives as undocumented immigrants. They were very open about their experiences. It had been more than 15 years since each had left Mexico for San Diego, having made the journey separately before meeting, and marrying, here. As we talked, Beatriz slowly began to cry. "I was afraid because I had never left home before," she said. "So when I was on my way here, I was very afraid. All the way from Manzanillo to Tijuana I cried—the whole way."

For Beatriz and others I talked with, leaving home was an important event. They separated themselves from family, friends, and community in Mexico to live in the United States as undocumented immigrants. The fundamental reason was work. A laborer can earn seven to ten times as much working on the U.S. side of the border as on the Mexican side. But there is more to the story than this. Personal histories of undocumented immigrants reveal a complex array of motives for migration. They provide insight into why Mexicans view migration to the United States as something within the realm of their possibilities. . . .

Migration as a Part of Family History
[Enrique][2]

As we sat and talked in his living room, Enrique Valenzuela told his story of coming to the United States. He was raised on a *rancho*—a very small agricultural community, usually consisting of only a few families, in the state of Puebla. . . . His family's land depended upon rainfall to grow corn and beans. "If it rains, there is work for six months. If it doesn't rain, there is no

---

Editor's Note: This case study was excerpted from *Shadowed Lives: Undocumented Immigrants in American Society* by Leo R. Chavez. In his study, Leo Chavez provides a description and analysis of the lives of undocumented workers in Southern California, particularly in San Diego County. Chavez has conducted research among legal and undocumented Mexican immigrants since 1980. Although there are many personal stories in *Shadowed Lives*, we have excerpted the stories of Beatriz and Enrique Valenzuela here.

[1]Leo R. Chavez, "The Valenzuela Family" from *Shadowed Lives: Undocumented Immigrants in American Society.* Copyright © 1992 by Holt, Rinehart and Winston. Reprinted with the permission of the publishers.

[2]Text in brackets was added for clarification.

work." During periods of little or no work, his father migrated elsewhere, including the United States, to earn money.

His father worked in the U.S. under the contract labor program known as the "Bracero Program." The term *bracero* is derived from *brazos*, or "arms," and refers to laborers, especially agricultural workers. In 1942, the U.S. government instituted the Bracero Program as a short-term solution to the agricultural labor shortage created by the influx of American men into the armed services during World War II. The program allowed American employers to hire, under contract, Mexican laborers for specific periods of time, usually a few months. Although it was originally a short-term program, the benefits of bracero labor resulted in the program's extension well beyond the war years. It was finally phased out in 1964. Over this 22-year period, hundreds of thousands of Mexicans were hired to work temporarily in the United States (Craig 1971).

Enrique's father worked as a bracero for 12 years. "Sometimes he'd get a contract for three months, six months, and then he would return to the rancho, to Mexico. And then the next year he would return [to the United States] again. He did that until the Bracero Program ended." During this time, Enrique worked on the rancho. He was the oldest child and as such, he said, "[from the time] I was very young, I had to work to help feed my brothers and sisters and mother."

In 1963, when he was 16, Enrique decided to leave the rancho because "there was no work there. We were very hungry. We earned enough to barely get by. But I wanted to do better, to get out of poverty, to do something with my life." And so Enrique migrated to Mexico City, where he found a job in the market selling tomatoes and chiles for 50 pesos (about four U.S. dollars) a week. After two months, he found a better job in a small factory, making car accessories such as antennas and mirrors. When he left that job, in 1970, he was earning about 275 pesos a week (about $22 U.S.).

After working in Mexico City for the same employer for nearly seven years, Enrique felt he needed a change. "I only earned enough to eat with and pay rent." He remembered his father talking about work in the United States. "My father would say that when it was good, you could get ahead. And that's how later I thought that someday I would come to this country." After the Bracero Program ended in 1964, Enrique's father continued to migrate to the United States as an undocumented worker, relying on contacts made with employers during his years as a bracero. His father always tried, however, both in person and in his letters to Enrique, to discourage Enrique's interest in migrating to the United States, "My father had told me that it was very hard and that he suffered a lot. 'When you first come to this country you suffer,' he would tell me. He tried not to have me come here."

In 1970, his father was working on a ranch in northern San Diego County. Enrique decided to take advantage of the situation, and convinced his father to help him migrate. Before leaving, Enrique had to inform his employer, who tried to dissuade him from pursuing his plans.

> I told my boss that I was going to come and try my luck here. He didn't like that. He told me Mexicans were not wanted here [in the United States] and that I would be treated very poorly. He said that with him I would have work for a lifetime, that it would not work out for me here and that I would never progress. So I told him that I wanted to try my luck because I had been with him for seven years and could not do anything more. So he got mad at me.

Despite his employer's objections and warnings, Enrique migrated to San Diego. He was 23 years old. . . .

Migration as a Part of Family History
[Beatriz]

Beatriz was in her mid-forties and had the tired look of someone who regularly worked long days. She showed a sly sense of humor when she spoke. She was born and raised in Manzanillo, Colima, where her family owned a large bakery. Because of the family business, Beatriz was able to study through high school. But in 1964, when Beatriz was 20 years old, her father died, setting off a period of bitter conflict between her and her two older brothers, who believed they alone were entitled to their father's inheritance. Beatriz believed that her brothers, especially the oldest one, were taking advantage of her since she was the youngest child. She believed that she, too, deserved some of the inheritance. This led to a period of intense conflict, which eventually caused her to leave for the United States.

> We were feuding, especially with my oldest brother. I didn't fight with my sisters because they were already married. But it was with the two boys that I fought every day. My oldest brother kicked me out of the house. He would kick me out just like that, saying "Leave my house," because the house was left in his name. We lived in a very large house.

During this time, Beatriz had friends whose married sisters lived in the United States but often returned to Manzanillo. "They would tell me about the United States and invite me to go back with them." Beatriz declined their invitations until finally the pressure of feuding with her brothers became too much to bear.

> I tolerated them [her brothers] for five years, but only for my mother, only for her. I would tell her that I wanted to go to another place or come here [the United States], and she would start to cry. When I couldn't stand it anymore, that's when I asked her for permission to come here.

Beatriz did not migrate to the United States for economic reasons. Family conflict drove her out of her home. "If it hadn't been for the problems with my brothers I wouldn't have to come here because I worked in our own business." She received advice and encouragement from her friends, who arranged for a place in the U.S. for Beatriz to stay and told her their relatives would assist her in finding work. She accepted their help but "they didn't know about my family problems because I didn't talk about that with anyone." Beatriz's memory of her trip from Manzanillo to Tijuana recalls the loneliness and fear felt by someone who had never left home before. "I was afraid and I would think of my mother. So the whole way I cried." When I heard her story, it had been about 17 years since Beatriz had last seen her mother.

. . .

Crossing over the hills and through the canyons presents risks that some individuals and families attempt to avoid. Various strategies attempt to blend illegal border crossers in with the thousands of people who daily cross legally at the official port of entry. Many apply for a temporary visiting permit, or shopping card, and use it as a pass across the border, staying beyond the time limitations. Beatriz, Enrique Valenzuela's wife, entered with such a card. As she remembered,

> I applied for a permit to cross. I went to Guadalajara and . . . they gave me a permit. So I came with a friend of mine. We got to Tijuana and . . . a sister of hers picked us up. My friend also had a permit. So there in San Ysidro they stamped our permits and we crossed. I came here on August 2, 1969.

Beatriz has returned to Mexico only once, for a few days in Tijuana in 1972 to have her first child. She has not been back since. As we sat on her sofa talking, Beatriz cried as she spoke of her longing to see her mother.

> During all these years I wanted to go but I am afraid of crossing the border and won't risk it. You know how they say that they assault people, murder women. I'm scared of crossing and that's why I don't go to Mexico. That's my problem.

Like Beatriz, many undocumented immigrants fear recrossing the border. This puts pressure on them to stay in the United States until they are sure they want, or are forced, to return home. This seems especially true for women, who very often immigrate on their first and only trip to the United States.

Perhaps realizing the desire to avoid the dangers associated with crossing the border, coyotes [border guides] also offer relatively safe passage by providing shopping cards that have been lost or stolen. Or, they make arrangements for women and children to pass through with other persons, particularly Americans, who make unlikely suspects for transporting illegal border crossers.

Beatriz found herself in need of such services in 1972, when she was ready to return to the U.S. after having her baby in a Tijuana hotel.

> I was in Tijuana and because I couldn't stay there my friend found someone to cross us. She sent a very young American guy. One of those guys who doesn't work, but wants money. He came after me and brought us. I didn't have any problems. They just asked him where we were headed. He said San Diego and they let us through without problems. That was the only time I left here [San Diego], but it was out of necessity.

. . .

Beatriz arrived in San Diego, she stayed with the sister of a friend she had come with. After finding a job as a live-in maid, Beatriz would visit her friend on weekends. Her friend worked for an older American woman in a large house with a swimming pool. "This woman would drink a lot, night and day. On the weekends, those of us who didn't have a place to stay would get together there and the lady didn't mind."

Beatriz's friend would sometimes invite male friends over to go swimming. On one of these occasions, Beatriz met Daniel. "Later, on the beach in downtown La Jolla, it's called The Cove, Daniel introduced Enrique to us. From there, we started to go out together. He would invite me to go out to eat, and to just be out because we didn't have money. He didn't and I didn't. I sent my $27 a week [all her earnings] to my mother." Enrique and Beatriz did not have much time to spend together. She worked as a live-in maid during the week and on some Sundays cleaned another house in order to earn an additional ten dollars, which she would keep for spending money.

Their relationship grew despite having little time to actually be together. As Beatriz tells it: "When I met him I didn't live with him. I only went to see him on weekends because I lived at my job and he with his friends, until I got pregnant with Carolina. That's when we looked for our own place, apart from our friends." They married in 1977, a year after their son was born.

. . .

The Steady Worker

Enrique typically is the first one to arrive at the Chinese restaurant where he works. He unlocks the kitchen door, straightens up a bit, and begins preparing the vegetables and meats to be used in the day's Cantonese and Mandarin dishes. It is a routine he knows well. He has worked for the same employer since he arrived in the United States in 1970, some 16 years by the time I met him in 1986. "For 15, 16 years, it is the same schedule. I go in at 10:30 A.M., and leave [the restaurant] at 9:45 or 10 at night. I return home and I arrive at 10:10 or 10:15 P.M. I am away from home for almost 12 hours."

Although Enrique had come to join his father, the owner of the farm where his father worked did not need more employees. And so he had the coyote drive him to La Jolla, where his father had heard that there was restaurant work available. He walked into the first restaurant he saw and asked for work. He was hired as a dishwasher part time, which was enough for Enrique to survive, but barely. "When I began sixteen years ago, it went very bad for me. I only worked three hours per day. I earned $1.50 per hour. The money was only enough to eat and pay the rent. There was no money for anything else. One year, exactly, I earned that salary. After one year, I earned $300 per month. For me, it was much better."

Full-time employment also meant Enrique had to experience a great American tradition: taxes. At this time it was easy for anyone to obtain a social security card, a practice that would change in later years. "My boss told me that in this country one had to pay the government. So I went to apply for my social security card. I began to pay taxes in 1971 and I have done so ever since."

Enrique gradually learned to prepare Chinese food. "When I first began, I washed dishes. They graduated me to cut vegetables. Next to cut meats. Later to a position to fry foods. Then another position to prepare and cook. To date, I am at that same position." The evolution of his skills improved his position at work. He now works on a salary rather than by the hour, earning between $900 and $1,000 a month, depending on tips.

Enrique's acquisition of skills in the kitchen has helped him weather changes at the restaurant. In 1974, his employer opened a new Chinese restaurant east of downtown and eventually closed the La Jolla restaurant. Enrique continued to work at the new restaurant. Enrique has also managed to continue working despite personnel shifts at the restaurant. Once, the majority of kitchen help were Mexican. According to Enrique, "The Chinese bring their families little by little. So, they begin to employ their relatives and cut down on the number of Mexicans. Right now there are very few of us Mexicans, four or five." Enrique attributes his continued employment to hard work. "In all these years, I've never failed to go to work because of a stomachache or headache. They notice that and so they give me a chance. I'm the only Mexican there who gets a paid vacation. They give me a week a year."

Enrique realizes that he has little economic mobility left at his job. He is earning about the best he could possibly earn at the restaurant. He also realizes that despite having worked for so many years at this job, his job is not necessarily permanent. He also does not receive any other benefits, although he is able to buy medical insurance at a reduced rate through his work. And over the years, he has experienced many personal slights and often has had to reduce his expectations. But he has endured all of this because at least the work was steady. He also believed he had only limited opportunities elsewhere due to his undocumented status.

> Without papers you have to tolerate everything at a job: humiliations, low wages, long hours. But if you leave that job and go to another, it's the same thing because you don't have papers. So for us, our papers are the most important thing in order to get ahead in this country. We want to progress. With papers we can open a cafeteria, for example, or a taco stand, where we can earn more, because we are not educated enough to find a good job. But we do like to work a lot.

A few months after Enrique arrived in San Diego, he met Beatriz, who was working as a live-in maid. They soon married, and began a family. Beatriz's pregnancy presented Enrique and Beatriz with some important economic problems, especially as to where Beatriz would deliver the baby. As Enrique said, "I had very little money saved. You know how it is when you arrive here without knowing anyone. They don't trust you without having credit or anything. So we thought that she should have the baby in Tijuana because it was more affordable. She went to Tijuana to give birth and she returned about ten days later with her [daughter]."

With the return of his wife and daughter, Enrique now had a family of three in San Diego. He became concerned with his family's future. Faced with limited economic mobility at their jobs, Enrique and Beatriz embarked on a strategy of saving what they could from their earnings. According to Enrique, "It was around that time that we started to save, not enough because we were now three. But because we were ambitious to accomplish something, we tried very hard." The concern with providing for a growing family and saving for a better future put added pressure on both Enrique and Beatriz to stay at their jobs, work hard, and not take the unnecessary risks associated with frequent job changes.

Beatriz's work history in San Diego did not begin when she met Enrique. After her tearful bus ride from her mother's home and the family bakery she had worked in, she too had to find work in San Diego. Undocumented Mexican women in San Diego work in many types of jobs, including manufacturing, the garment industry, and restaurants. Many, however, are engaged in domestic work, as live-in babysitters, live-in housekeepers or maids, and housekeepers who service a number of houses a week. Beatriz's story, and that of other Mexican women, suggests that this type of work is not "natural" in the sense that women may not have had any particular training for it. On the contrary, their past work experiences may have been as varied as that of men. But faced with limited opportunities in the San Diego job market, immigrant women turn to domestic work. And at times, they view it as having strategic advantages for them in comparison to other types of jobs they might find.

Women and Domestic Work

Beatriz arrived in San Diego on August 2, 1969, a day she remembers well. She arrived at the house of her traveling companion's sister. After a couple of days' rest, her friend's sister helped her find work as a live-in maid in La Jolla. The job paid little, the work load was heavy, and she had little time off. "I started working for a family that had three girls and two adults. But I was overworked there. All day, until 1 A.M., I would be ironing for only 27 dollars a week. I got half a day on Sundays off. On Sundays, after feeding them breakfast, I would go out and then I would have to be back that same day because if I came back the next morning they would reduce my pay."

Beatriz left that job after six months. She found another that paid slightly better, 30 dollars a week, but the lady she worked for moved to Colorado. Without work, she stayed with a friend until she found work again. She continued to work as a live-in maid until her daughter was born in 1972, after which Beatriz decided being away from home all week would be too difficult. Her friend, who also worked as a housekeeper, had already been in the United States about thirteen years at that point and helped her find day work through her employer's friends. In this way she found her first daytime housecleaning job. This led to additional jobs.

After I had Carolina, I went to work with [that family]. The lady liked the way I worked. I first started to work only one day a week with her because I had just gotten out of the hospital. She liked the way I worked so much that she gave me another day. I told her that I only had these two days of work and that I needed more. She got me work with an architect. That architect gave me two days, too. The lady next door to my first employer also asked me if I could work for her, and I said "Yes." She gave me one day, so I worked the five days.

After five years, Beatriz stopped working for the architect and the neighbor, and found two new employers to fill out her week. By 1986, she had worked for these two new employers for ten years and in her original household for 15 years. Over this time she has seen her pay for a five and a half to six hour day go from 10 to 12 to 14 dollars a day, until finally she was earning about 27 dollars a day in 1986 and 1987.

Over the years Beatriz has developed what she considers to be a personal relationship with her employers. Indeed, she has exchanged formal benefits and a contractual work relationship for this informal arrangement based upon personal relationships. Beatriz acknowledges that the lack of formal benefits, particularly medical insurance, is difficult. Although Enrique has medical insurance, it does not cover Beatriz and their children. "The day I get sick, it's expensive." She has come to depend upon an informal agreement for limited benefits.

When I get sick and don't work, I get paid. Holidays I get paid. If I have a school meeting for the kids, I still get paid. Lots of times I've been sick and they've given me half the money so I can go to the doctor. And they treat me well. They don't give me too much work.

The fact that Beatriz has worked so many years for the same employers has allowed her to develop a personal relationship in which the informal benefits are understood and abided by. Other women do not develop such a relationship with an employer. Women who clean various houses a week typically get paid only on the days they work. They are, in essence, independent contractors. Their relationships with employers are more limited, and they often have many employers, some long-term but many on a short-term basis.

. . .

As Beatriz noted,

When my kids are sick, I tell the lady that my youngest child is sick and she'll tell me to leave right away, even if I've worked for only an hour. She'll say that it's more important to be with your son than work. So, that's why I'm happy working there. They never check when I get there or when I leave . . . If I worked in a factory or laundromat, my hours would be controlled. I would have to be there at a certain hour and leave at a certain hour. Work the eight hours. I like working in homes . . . I can go whenever I want and leave when my kids need me. In a factory I wouldn't have that advantage. If my kids were sick I'd still have to go to work."

. . .

Learning to Live as an "Illegal Alien"

. . . Enrique Valenzuela describes his many years in San Diego as similar to being in jail.

> In all these 16 years I feel like I've been in jail. I don't feel free. I came to this country to work, not to do things on the street that you shouldn't do. That's not what I mean by freedom. I'm referring to the feeling of being in a prison because if you go out, like when we go out for fun, it's always in the back of your mind, will immigration show up? Or when you go to work you think all the time, from the moment you walk out of your home, you think, "Will the immigration stop me on the way or when I'm at work?" So I do feel like I'm in jail.

As Enrique and I talked about his feeling of being in jail, a song popular at the time, "Jaula de Oro" ("The Gilded Cage"),[3] came up in our conversation. He felt the song echoed his situation, and that of many undocumented immigrants who have been in the United States for many years. Two of the verses are particularly apt here:

Aquí estoy establecido en los Estados Unidos. Diez años pasaron ya en que cruzé de mojado. Papeles no me he arreglado sigo siendo ilegal.	Here I am established in the United States. It's been ten years since I crossed as a wetback. I never applied for papers, I'm still illegal.
¿De qué me sirve el dinero si yo soy como prisionero dentro de esta gran nación? Cuando me acuerdo hasta lloro aunque la jaula sea de oro, no deja de ser prisión.	What good is money if I am like a prisoner in this great nation? When I think about it, I cry. Even if the cage is made of gold, it doesn't make it less a prison.

Enrique believed that the song described his situation to a degree. But he wanted to make it clear that when the singer speaks of "gold," it does not mean that he is rich. It merely means that he has a job and an income. "I don't feel free, but we don't have a lot of money, either."

All these statements have in common the idea of being encapsulated within a larger social system. Describing themselves as being in jail, living within in a circle or a chicken coop, and feeling confined within San Diego's borders are all ways of relating how their undocumented status places limits on their incorporation into society. Although they work and live in San Diego, their movements are ultimately constrained. Their agreement on a lack of freedom of movement emphasizes that even though they are inside a larger social system, they are not fully part of that social system. Their incorporation has not been complete.

Home as a Refuge

To allay some of the constant fear of apprehension and deportation, undocumented immigrants attempt to create some security through a network of friends and relatives. They tend to live near relatives and friends who had

---

[3]"Jaula de Oro," performed by Los Tigres del Norte, produced by Profono Internacional Inc. 1985.

previously migrated, or people who they themselves helped to migrate and become established in the area. But at the heart of this attempt to create some sense of security is their home, which becomes a retreat, a place of refuge, a sanctuary in which they are less visible than on the streets or at work.

For Beatriz and Enrique Valenzuela, being home offers some relief from their daily fears. Beatriz leaves home as the sun rises and walks about ten blocks to the bus stop. She has been robbed of her bus money twice while walking along the road. She then rides a series of buses to arrive in La Jolla, a trip that takes about an hour and a half. She returns late in the afternoon. Enrique leaves for work at about 10 A.M. and returns home at about 10:30 at night. During the week, Enrique rarely is able to talk with his family. His daughter and son both attend school during the day. On Sundays, the Valuenzuela family finally has the opportunity to interact with one another.

With their family outside of the home most of time, Enrique and Beatriz constantly worry about one of the family being apprehended. Only when they are all at home do they feel a sense of security. As Beatriz said, "When one is at home, one feels secure. We are always concerned with the danger of the immigration [agents] on the bus. I'm always in danger. When I arrive home, it's then that I can rest and feel content. Because there is always fear of walking the streets." Enrique agreed:

> When we are all at home, [Sunday], is the only day that we are all happy, because it is that day that we all feel very secure, secure no matter what the danger. My wife is the first to leave. When she leaves the fear begins. Then, when my children leave, the same fear. Finally, when I leave, well all day long while I am at work, it is all I think about, that something could happen to us, because of the status that we have in this country.

Enrique and Beatriz carry these fears around with them during the day. Although Enrique has never been apprehended, he still becomes full of fear when he spots an immigration officer. Enrique and Beatriz believe that everything they have managed to acquire over almost two decades in the United States could easily be lost. In 1979, they purchased a modest two-bedroom home in a low-income area. They have appliances, a television, a car. And yet they realize that they live in a house of cards that could easily come tumbling down. As Enrique said, "At night I dream about it, that they catch me. That everything caves in." Beatriz added, "It's true. You're terrorized. I have nightmares!"

Once again, the song "Jaula de Oro" speaks to the fears held by undocumented immigrants and the security they often seek in seclusion:

De mi trabajo a mi casa. Yo no sé lo que me pasa aunque soy hombre de hogar. Casi no salgo a la calle pues tengo miedo que me hallen y me puedan deportar.

From my job to my home. I don't know what is happening to me. I am a homebody. I almost never go out to the street. I am afraid I will be found and could be deported.

For many undocumented immigrants who have formed a family in the United States, such as Enrique and Beatriz, one of their greatest fears is that a family member might be apprehended. When a spouse or child is late coming home, the fear quickly sets in that the person has been apprehended. Wives who do not work, and who do not have a great deal of experience interacting with the larger society, are particularly fearful of their husband's sudden apprehension.

. . .

When undocumented immigrants are apprehended, they often experience a great deal of pressure to sign a voluntary departure form. When a person becomes defiant, as did Beatriz Valenzuela, the pressure can mount. Beatriz's experience reveals both the tragedy and the comedy of the situation.

Beatriz's greatest fear, for almost 18 years, had been that she would be apprehended while riding the bus to work in La Jolla. On July 9, 1986, that fear became a reality. During that week, the immigration authorities were boarding most of the buses entering La Jolla in search of "illegal aliens" who worked in the beach community's restaurants, hotels, and private homes. On that day, Beatriz's bus arrived on La Jolla Boulevard at about 6:40 A.M. With officers stationed at the doors in front and back of the bus to ensure no one could jump off, officers asked the occupants for their documents. Not having any, Beatriz was asked to get off the bus. Because they were interested in legalizing their status, Beatriz and Enrique had consulted a lawyer whose advice was not to sign a voluntary departure, but to ask for a court hearing. Armed with this knowledge, Beatriz was ready when the immigration agent suggested signing a voluntary departure.

> He took out a piece of paper and told me that we were going to fill it out right now, so you can sign it, so that you can go to Tijuana. I told him that I was not going to sign anything. Why should I? He said, "You aren't going to sign?" I said, "No." He said, "Do you know how many years await you in jail?" I said, "No." He said. "You can expect two or three years in jail." I said, "Really." He said, "Yes, really, and all because you don't want to sign this document. If you sign it right now, you'll be taken to Tijuana. But if you don't sign it, it will go real bad for you," I said, "Well, too bad. If you're going to feed me in jail and I don't have to work, then that's a vacation for me!"

The immigration agents took Beatriz to a detention center near the border, where she stayed for three days. Beatriz remembers it well, since one of those days was her birthday. Three days later Beatriz was released, after Enrique posted a $2,000 bond to guarantee that she would appear at a court hearing.

Carolina, Beatriz's oldest child, was 13 when her mother was pulled off the bus and detained. Carolina's reactions to the news of her mother's arrest reflects the confused fears of a young child, and her lack of experience with life in Mexico, the country of her birth. She said,

> I was worried that we were going to be sent back to Mexico, that we had to go back and live like those people, without any homes. They have to sleep in the streets, sell anything, like gum. There was going to be no food. Maybe I

> couldn't go to school because my parents needed money. . . . We were going to lose everything we had here. . . . I was afraid that maybe my brother [age 11] had to stay here, and we had to go, because he's an American citizen. And maybe the government would send him to some kind of shelter for kids that don't have homes or anything. Maybe he was going to miss his parents and me.

Carolina's fears pictured the worst-case scenario, much of which was based on stereotypes of the poverty which exists in Tijuana. But even given that her depiction of possible events may not have been realistic, it was a very vivid image in her mind. She suddenly found the future security of her home and family in doubt. She was caught up in events over which she had no control and little understanding. The only thing she knew at the time was that her life had the possibility of being turned upside-down, changing from one of hope to one of despair. Carolina's fears of her brother's separation from the family because of his different status—born in the United States and therefore a U.S. citizen—reflects the types of stress found in binational families.

. . .

Because of their desire to legalize their status, undocumented immigrants seek out lawyers and immigration consultants, sometimes with disastrous consequences, as with Enrique and Beatriz Valenzuela.

In 1976, after their son José was born in San Diego, Enrique and Beatriz sought legal advice on legalizing their status. They had heard that a U.S. citizen child could apply to have his or her parents enter the country as legal immigrants. Unfortunately, the law had changed so that a child must be 21 years old before being able to assist his or her parents to immigrate legally.

The "lawyer" they sought out had been recommended by a friend. As Enrique said, since the law had changed, "The lawyer, who said he was a lawyer, said he couldn't do anything more. The only thing was to wait for amnesty." For amnesty for Enrique, Beatriz, and their daughter Carolina, the "lawyer" charged them $700, with half due immediately, and the rest after the case was completed. According to Enrique, "From 1977 to 1980–81, he couldn't do anything. Amnesty wasn't getting here."

Enrique then asked him if there was any other way to legalize his family's status. "He said that there was another way, but it was expensive. He said that it came to about $5,000. I asked if it was a sure way. He said that in 90 percent of the cases it was. He said that we had been here a long time and it would be possible. I told him that we had some money saved, but it was all that we had."

Enrique gave the "lawyer" $1,000 that day. He then arranged to pay $200 a month until he paid $2,500. The other half would be due when the case was over. However, there arose additional expenses in the case for which the "lawyer" needed more money. "He said if you don't pay more then that's the end of everything, and you lose all you've put into it [the case]." Enrique and Beatriz believed that something was wrong, since the initial agreement was to only pay half of the total cost before the case was settled. But they paid nonetheless. The reason: fear. As Enrique noted,

> The man didn't threaten me, but we were afraid. When he required the second half from me, after I had paid him the first, we were very afraid. So we continued paying. Not so much for ourselves, because we knew he was cheating us, but because if we didn't finish paying he would denounce us [to the immigration authorities].

Two years later, Enrique confronted the "lawyer." Enrique was angry because nothing had been done and he had paid everything requested of him. The man's response, according to Enrique, was that "It was a matter for the courts, they should be calling us."

As it turned out, Enrique soon found out that the "lawyer" had a partner, another lawyer, who was also involved in the case. When this second lawyer died shortly after Enrique's confrontation with his original "lawyer," he found his case had been taken over by yet another lawyer. At this point the original "lawyer" directed Enrique to see the new lawyer about his case. "He now didn't have any more to do with my case."

Enrique went to the new lawyer and found out something surprising and disturbing. Virtually nothing had been done on his case. There were no legal papers filed (so the court would not be "calling"). Moreover, "We thought he was a lawyer, but later when he told us that he couldn't continue our case any longer and sent us to another lawyer, it was the other lawyer who told us that he wasn't a lawyer. He was a notary public." The real lawyer, who had died, was actually the lawyer of record on the case.

As we sat in his living room, the center of the only island of security he had in San Diego, Enrique just shook his head in disbelief. He had sought to increase his security, and instead became a victim of those who prey on the misfortunes of others. As he said, "It's not fair that they steal from us in this way without doing anything. We earn our money as quickly as we can and it is not much that we can save. It's easy for them to take it away quickly." Beatriz was clearly angry when she reflected on the years they were involved with this person and the money they spent:

> In order to meet his installments we had to cut back and deny ourselves other things that we needed, for us and our children. We had to pay $200 every month, every month. It made me sick to think that over here we had to limit ourselves a lot because of him, and it's not fair.

Unfortunately, Enrique and Beatriz's experience is not uncommon. Undocumented immigrants who have lived in the United States for many years, have families, and fear that detection and apprehension will destroy everything they have worked for, provide easy targets for schemers who dangle the dream of security that comes with documentation. Enrique and Beatriz's experience was just one of the many, sometimes bitter, lessons undocumented immigrants encounter as they learn to live in the United States.

. . .

Immigrant Children

Carolina Valenzuela had been born in Tijuana but was raised in San Diego since a few days after birth. Although she and her friends, some of them recently arrived from Mexico, rarely discuss their immigration status openly, she is certain that all her friends believe she is a U.S. citizen.

> I've told everybody I'm an American citizen, that I was born here. On applications, I just put I was born in the U.S.A. So all my friends know I'm a U.S. citizen. But I just lie. . . . And I think I have friends that lie just like me. . . . I'd rather say I'm American born because I feel I have more rights. . . . I feel more comfortable saying I'm an American citizen, like I could go to any college. . . . I have more opportunities.

Carolina participates as a citizen in various school activities. When I first met her in 1986, she was in her first year of high school and a member of the campus Reserve Officer Training Corps (ROTC). The year before that, she had been one of four students (out of about 300) chosen to speak at her eighth-grade graduation ceremony. She was the only Latina so chosen, an honor she believes she would not have received had it been known she was an "illegal alien." Through their children's activities, such as Carolina's, undocumented parents are drawn into the larger society.

. . .

[Carolina] had been raised in San Diego since infancy and her [Beatriz's] ten-year-old son had been born in the city. When considering taking her children back to Mexico to live, she said, "You can only imagine the brutal change they would face. First of all, our children would lose their friendships, school, customs, food, manner of dress. For them, it would be terrible." Beatriz likened such an experience to a plant being pulled out of the ground by its roots. "The roots are here and it's like ripping a tree out of the ground and taking it over there. Can you imagine those roots? By the time they got there, they would be practically dead."

. . .

Enrique and Beatriz Valenzuela also see more opportunities for their children in the United States. They view education as an important key to mobility, as Beatriz noted:

> I think that our children do have more opportunities here for an education, to study, to have what I didn't have. I didn't get an education in Mexico, but we worked and worked so that they would have more opportunities than we had. And that's why I want them to study and study hard so that they won't have to work as hard as we did.

Unfortunately, life does not always proceed as desired. Three years after this interview, the Valenzuela's daughter, Carolina, became pregnant, dropped out of high school and moved in with her boyfriend. Given that she was a very good student, her parents hold onto the hope that she will eventually finish her education.

QUESTIONS FOR DISCUSSION AND ANALYSIS

Historically and Geographically/Globally Contextual

1. What historical policies in the 20th-century United States have been directed toward Mexican immigrants?
2. How are these policies reflected across the generations of this family? How is Enrique's life different from and similar to his father's life? How is Beatriz's life different from and similar to Carolina's life? How would Beatriz's and Enrique's lives be different if they were legal immigrants in California? Would Beatriz and Enrique have made different choices for themselves and their family if the Bracero Program still existed?
3. What new political debates, policies, and assistance programs for legal and illegal immigrants have most likely affected the Valenzuelas in the years since Chavez interviewed them?
4. What negative ideologies or controlling images do Enrique, Beatriz, or their children confront? Trace the historical development of these ideologies.

Socially Constructed

5. Do we know anything about Enrique, Beatriz, or Carolina in terms of their sexuality? If so, what do we know? What don't we know?
6. Why does Carolina deny to her friends that she is Mexican by birth? What are the consequences for her? If her response is a common survival strategy among the children of Mexican immigrants, how might that strategy shape future group identity and political actions?
7. Why did some of Beatriz's early employers dock her pay if she came to work in the morning, rather than spending the night in their household?
8. What is Enrique's conception of work? How does it fit with the ideology of the "American Dream"?
9. Does the Valenzuelas' success in this country challenge structures of race, class, gender, and sexuality? Does their success reinforce dominant assumptions? How?
10. Are Enrique and Beatriz likely candidates to join a union? Why?
11. How might the meaning of race, class, gender, and sexuality in their lives be different if they were working-class residents of California? How does immigration construct these inequalities differently?

Power Relationships

12. Beatriz's working so many years for the same employers has allowed her to develop a personal relationship in which informal benefits are understood and abided by. What are some of these informal benefits? How does Beatriz's position compare to that of other women employed in domestic service? What are some of the reasons that Beatriz is *still* in a precarious position at work?

13. Why is fear a central part of the Valenzuelas' lives? What are some of the things they fear? How are their fears related to their social locations?

14. Discuss the power relationships between employers, Beatriz, and Enrique. In what ways do Beatriz and Enrique have power over their work experiences? Do Beatriz or Enrique desire to resist exploitation of their labor by their employers? Do they resist unfavorable conditions at work? How?

15. We hear nothing about the sexuality of the Valenzuelas until the discussion of Beatriz's and Carolina's accidental pregnancies. What kinds of birth control might have been available to Beatriz and Carolina? What barriers to effective use of birth control might they have experienced? How might their social location put them at greater risk for accidental pregnancy?

Macro/Social Structural and Micro/Social Psychological Levels

16. Describe how macro structures (i.e., economic institutions, government, educational systems, etc.) have influenced the Valenzuelas' lives in the United States. How have they both benefited and suffered from macro structural influences? What are some of the ways they have learned to negotiate these structures?

17. Technically it is illegal for individuals like Beatriz or Enrique to live in California, yet what social groups benefit the most from having undocumented immigrants in the United States? Why?

18. Language is never mentioned as a structural constraint for either Enrique or Beatriz. Discuss how language could have affected the Valenzuelas' lives.

19. What are the "multiple truths" that surface around the Valenzuelas' situation? How might a wealthy employer view Beatriz's family situation or illegal immigrant status? How might teachers view Carolina's unintended pregnancy? How might the Valenzuela children view their parents?

20. Why is it so common for undocumented immigrants like Beatriz and Enrique to work in restaurants and hotels, within private homes, or on farms? Discuss the macro forces that make this the case as well as the individual reasons people like Beatriz or Enrique might have for taking these kinds of jobs.

21. How has Carolina's success in the education system privileged her? How might her life have been different if she had never lied about her immigrant status?

Simultaneously Expressed

22. What social characteristics or dimensions of inequality seem more prominent in the Valenzuelas' situation? Which seem less apparent? Why?

23. How do race, class, gender, and sexuality shape Beatriz's, Enrique's, and Carolina's lives differently?
24. How does race affect Beatriz's, Enrique's, and Carolina's lives? Does it affect them in the same ways? Different ways?
25. What impact do sexuality and gender have on the Valenzuelas' life experiences? (For example, if Carolina had been a lesbian or male, how might her life have been different? If Enrique had been caught by the immigration services rather than Beatriz, would he have been treated differently?)
26. If Beatriz had been Puerto Rican, how might her life have been different?

Implications for Social Action and Social Justice

27. Where does this story lead us? What can we learn from it about the experiences of illegal immigrants? What will it take to improve life for families like the Valenzuelas?
28. If we could take this vignette and create one policy that might improve the Valenzuelas' current situation, what would it be and how would we implement it?
29. What kinds of resistance benefited Beatriz, Enrique, or Carolina? What can we learn from their actions?

REFERENCES

Bean, Frank D., Rodolfo O. de la Garza, Bryan R. Roberts, and Sidney Weintraub (Eds.). 1997. *At the Crossroads: Mexican Migration and U.S. Policy.* Lanham, MD: Rowman and Littlefield.

Brebenner, Candice Lewis. 1998. *A Nationality of Her Own: Women, Marriage, and the Law of Citizenship.* Berkeley, CA: University of California Press.

Chavez, Leo R. 1992. *Shadowed Lives: Undocumented Immigrants in American Society.* Fort Worth, TX: Harcourt Brace.

——— 1998. *Shadowed Lives: Undocumented Immigrants in American Society.* Second Edition. Fort Worth, TX. Harcourt Brace.

Del Castillo, Richard G. and Arnoldo de León. 1996. *North to Aztlán: A History of Mexican Americans in the United States.* New York: Twayne Publishers.

Hondagneu-Sotelo, Pierrette. 1994. *Gendered Transitions: Mexican Experiences of Immigration.* Berkeley, CA: University of California Press.

Jacobsen, David. 1998. *The Immigration Reader: America in a Multidisciplinary Perspective.* Malden, MA: Blackwell.

Maciel, David R. and María Herrera-Sobek (Eds.). 1998. *Culture Across Borders: Mexican Immigration and Popular Culture.* Tucson, AZ: The University of Arizona Press.

Romero, Mary, Pierrette Hondagneu-Sotelo and Vilma Ortiz (Eds.). 1997. *Challenging Fronteras: Structuring Latina and Latino Lives in the U.S.* New York: Routledge.

Ruiz, Vicki L. 1998. *From Out of the Shadows: Mexican Women in Twentieth-Century America.* New York: Oxford University Press.

Torre, Adela de la and Beatríz M. Pesquera (Eds.). 1993. *Building with Our Hands: New Directions in Chicana Studies.* Berkeley, CA: University of California Press.